MW01206589

The Prepper's Guide to Surviving the End of the World, as We Know It

M.D. Creekmore

Copyright © 2015 M.D. Creekmore

All rights reserved. No part of this publication may be reproduced, stored
in or introduced into a retrieval system, or transmitted, in any form, or by
any means (electronic, mechanical, photocopying, recording, or
otherwise), without the prior written permission of the copyright holder.
To do otherwise is illegal and punishable by law.

All information contained in this book is for educational purposes only.
The author shall not have any reliability or responsibility to any person or
entity with respect to any loss or damage caused, or allegedly caused by,
directly or indirectly by the information contained in this book.

ISBN-10: 1523408650

ISBN-13: 978-1523408658

DEDICATION

This book is dedicated to all of my readers at
TheSurvivalistBlog.net

CONTENTS

Chapter 1

INTRODUCTION – WHY I PREP

The reason most people do not prepare (other than the fact that they think it is just silly) is because they think that nothing will ever happen to them, and if it does, that the federal government will take care of them and their needs. After all the federal government has spent and continues to spend billions of taxpayer dollars on disaster preparations including stocked mega-bunkers and contingency plans.

However, what these people fail to realize is that those preps are being implemented by the federal government are not there to protect the general population; they are there to protect government officials and to ensure the continuity of the government. The federal government could care less about you as an individual.

The U.S. government has the resources and inside information that allows them to accurately foretell when a major disaster or complete collapse is coming weeks and sometimes even years in advance. And they have been prepping and building stocked underground bunkers on a mass scale. Despite the fact that our tax dollars are being used to build and stock these bunkers, you and I are not invited.

We will be on our own if anything worse than a regional natural disaster strike. We will have to provide for and protect ourselves after any major disruption such as an economic collapse, EMP or pandemic.

What do I think is the most likely SHTF event? I don't think any one problem or event will cause the collapse of the American empire. It is more likely that a number of separate but interlocking events and issues will lead to a decline, or as I now believe, a complete collapse on a scale not seen since the fall of the Roman Empire.

In fact, many of the same types of issues that plagued the Roman Empire for decades before its final fall are also the same issues that are currently threatening the United States and much of the industrialized world. What most people fail to realize is the fact that the collapse is happening right now, and has been going on for several decades.

Rome was not built in a day and it did not collapse overnight. Think of the current ongoing collapse of the United States as a very slow moving a domino effect; the problem is that we are now growing closer to the last domino, and the closer we get the faster each will fall.

Free Trade with Communist China

Communist China is not our friend and has overtaken the U.S. economically. China will be in a position to surpass the U.S. militarily within the next ten years. Yet we continue to import, buy and consume products from China by the millions every day. In fact, it is getting more and more difficult to buy anything in the U.S. that does not have the "made in china" label attached to it. U.S. goods and private services trade with China totaled $439 billion in imports 2012.

Meanwhile, China uses those funds to build its military might and expand its military technology. The U.S has even been selling and giving china advanced technology that can be used against the U.S. in a military confrontation. A large portion of that technology has passed from the U.S. to Israel and then from Israel on to China.

In 2012, a pentagon contractor was caught selling military technology to China (no doubt bought with funds that U.S. consumers of "made in China" products had sent them) according to the report they had sold China the software and engines needed to make its first-ever modern attack helicopter. This is only one incident and I am sure that there are many more of which we are unaware.

China also holds a huge sum in U.S. debt and could crash the dollar at any time by cashing in the over 1.1 trillion dollars it owns in U.S. bonds, flooding the global economy and driving the dollar's value down near zero.

A breakdown of the traditional family

America has turned from a nation promoting morality and faith in God to a nation where anything goes, with the most perverse and ungodly acts being accepted, promoted and even glorified by the media and "our" government.

In addition, if anyone disagrees or speaks out against this immorality he is labeled as promoting hate or bigotry, or as being a racist. This quickly shuts most opponents up while simultaneously implanting the message in everyone's mind that those acts in question should be accepted and are somehow normal.

A breakdown of morality

Everywhere we look, we (and our children) are bombarded with images of sex and obscenity in books, magazines, motion pictures, music, and TV. This constant bombardment has promoted promiscuity and has corrupted the minds of the American people. This has made us into a nation a degenerates and perverts.

According to a recent report by Maranathamrc.com, Americans spend 13.1 billion dollars on pornography every year, which according to the report is the same amount the country spends on foreign aid!

More than 260 million Internet pages are pornographic, an increase of 1,800% in just five years. Christian Broadcasting Network said,

"We're living in a sex-saturated society. Even the popular culture is often pulsing to a pornographic beat. Clothing that was seen only in porn magazines decades ago now drapes some of our most celebrated pop icons."

A declining belief in God, the Bible, and Christian values

A recent report published at The Daily Mail, "Americans starting to lose faith?" says that the "Belief in God and miracles declines as Darwinism becomes more popular." The number of Americans who believe in God is declining, as a new poll shows a move away from traditional beliefs. The Harris poll, which questioned more than 2,250 adults about their beliefs, found that those with the strongest faith lived mostly in the South and voted Republican. The online poll also showed that more Americans were describing themselves at 'not very religious' and that there was an increase in those believing in Darwin's theory of evolution.

As a nation, we are turning away from God and the religious principles that this nation was built on. These founding principles have been what has held us together as a nation and kept us strong. But it seems that we are banning God from the country and our lives.

Declining Freedom and Turning Away from a Constitutional Government

We have been seeing a decline in freedom for a long time but after the attacks on 9-11 the loss personal freedom, privacy and constitutional rights have been on a rapid decline. Now we are constantly watched, monitored, and recorded. We can now legally be detained and held indefinitely without a trial or due process. In addition, U.S. citizens can be assassinated on U.S. soil by order of the president.

Just like the imaginary "war on drugs," the war on terror has been used as an excuse to trample on individual constitutional rights and to increase the power of the government (or, more precisely) the ultra-wealthy that control the country from behind the curtains). Scare the population enough and they will willingly turn over their freedom and rights for a promised margin of safety.

As has been said: and is practiced religiously by those in power) "never let a crisis go to waste." This is also the same tactic that the Obama administration tried to use to destroy the Second Amendment after Sandy Hook.

Militarization of Police Forces Nationwide

It seems that every day I read news reports of police abuse of power--everything from shooting and killing an unarmed and handcuffed man to shooting a suspect in the back while he tried to run away, or a man executed by police for camping on public land (all justified of course). I've read about police shooting and killing chained and caged dogs--even puppies and 5-pound Chihuahuas are not safe from these thugs in uniform.

Now to make matters worse, police departments around the country seem to be gearing up for war with military hardware and military tactics. Who do they plan on going to war with you ask? Well, the American people of course. Who else? We are already living in a police state under a "soft" form of martial law and they are getting ready to tighten the screws even tighter. That is why those in power are getting all of this in place.

A One Party Political System

Many Americans think that they have a choice when they enter the voting booth. Well, guess what...we do not. Republicans and Democrats, Democrats and Republicans. What is the difference?

Neither represents the American people; neither gives one big crap about defending individual rights or the Constitution.

In the U.S., we have a one-party system masquerading as a two-party system. This gives voters the illusion of choice and a hope for change. The problem is that both parties are controlled by the same people (the super rich who really run the country). The system is rigged and we do not have a choice.

Corruption of the Political System

See above. As former Governor of Minnesota, Jesse Ventura has said, when you spend millions of dollars to get elected to a position that pays a hundred thousand a year, you know those figures don't add up. They are all a bunch of crooks – money, ego and a hunger for power have corrupted the American political system.

"The truth is there are very few members [of the U.S. Congress] who I could even name or could think of who didn't at some level participate in that [system of bribery and corruption in Washington D.C.]." Jack Abramoff, professional lobbyist and onetime power broker for the elite of Washington, D.C. (during a CBS's 60 Minutes interview, Sunday, November 6, 2011).

School System Used to Indoctrinate Children

Government run school systems are nothing more than indoctrination centers for our children, a place where they can be groomed and molded into mindless automata who like the government. They are indoctrinated by propaganda designed by psychologists to make future generations of American citizens into subservient slaves in a Big Brother police state.

When I was going to school, I carried pocket knives. (So did other kids and no one got cut or murdered.) I even read gun magazines in the classroom and no one said anything, other than my teachers asking to take a look at the magazines after I was done. I think they

11

were just glad that I was reading something. I remember one boy bringing a slingshot to school and we set up a cardboard box and shot at it with the slingshot while the teachers watched.

Now schools are like a prison where everything and everyone is watched and monitored and any form of free expression is suppressed and quickly "corrected" with the latest political correctness propaganda. They are training children to be adults who view being constantly surveilled and monitored by "authorities" as normal and even welcomed and demanded by a subservient population.

They are also training children to be dumbed down adults that cannot think for themselves, to have no personal beliefs, thoughts or opinion other than what they are told by the "authorities" via the government controlled mainstream media.

"He alone, who owns the youth, gains the Future!"

— *Adolf Hitler, speech at the Reichsparteitag, 1935*

Please read – Hitler Youth… and Indoctrination by Our Public Schools.

A Government Controlled Mainstream Media via Newspapers, Magazines, Radio, Movies, and TV

The stuff that you see on broadcasts like CNN aren't news or reporting but the controlled media simply spewing forth talking points that have been provided for them by the white house and other government agencies. This has been admitted to by mainstream "news" organizations http://goo.gl/RRNly8.

> The corporate media is now openly admitting that they are in fact controlled stenographers that do nothing more than echo pre-scripted narratives outlined in talking

points created by the rulers of America's shadow government.

They use the mainstream corporate media to push their agenda and views and to persuade the American people to do and believe what they want them to do and believe all while believing that it is for their own good. They even convince people it was their own decision. This is mass media brainwashing http://goo.gl/01crVX and those in power are good at it.

> People as drones, as automatons, in some kind of mind-control stupor, while thinking they are living in a free society. I do not say this with disdain, but more as a matter of fact.

It is beyond belief that the federal government is declaring anyone who doesn't agree with government policies as having a psychiatric disorder.

Support the U.S. Constitution or disagree with government policy or the policy makers and you might have a psychiatric disorder. After all, according to B.O. we "wrongheaded" Americans who need to trust the government more—if America would just have more trust in the government everything would be peaches and cream.

Taking Control of the Internet

Just about the only semi-free media left is the Internet and that is why the federal government wants to control it. Currently, the Obama administration is about to introduce a Chinese-style ID program for everyone and a few other tweaks that will allow government agencies and their controllers to tighten their grip and control of everything done and said online http://goo.gl/IRgCcy.

> What Obama has done to free speech is kill it dead utilizing a bias-oriented justice system and governmental control. He has effectively put the gears forward to shut

down free speech on the Internet, and is now planning an, even more, erroneous putsch that will destroy freedom of expression completely. Plans are coming into place for a Chinese style thought control program called the "National Strategy for Trusted Identities in Cyberspace" which will force every internet user to completely give up their privacy, be labeled and tracked even further than is usual by the NSA.

In addition, we now have Democrats proposing trolling the media and the internet for "hate speech" http://goo.gl/KxWkwg which will be defined as whatever they say it is. Folks, it's all about control: control of everything you do, control of what you thing and control of what you say. The best way for those in power to do that is to have full control over all media outlets, including the Internet.

Political Correctness is Out of Control

You might be a racist if you have an American flag, don't like Mexican food, disagree with Obama's policies. It seems that the one 100% guaranteed way to know if you're a racist is to look in the mirror: if you see a white person looking back at you, then you're a racist. Because only white people can be racist.

This seems to be the general assumption made by the mainstream media and race-baiters, like Al Sharpton, who would probably call me a racist—all because I keep white leghorn hens or perhaps because I own two black giant hens. Who knows what he would say, but one thing is certain he would probably find a way to make it about color and the mainstream would be all over it.

By now, I'm sure, that you have heard about the LA clippers owner Donald Sterling and the racist comments that he made to his girlfriend during what he thought was a private conversation. While his comments were undoubtedly racist against blacks, those

14

comments are his personal views and no matter how wrong those comments might be or who those comments might offend, is he not entitled to his beliefs? Does he not have a right to express those beliefs in a "private" conversation?

Apparently not, at least according to the NBA, the players, the media, and fans nationwide. Because of his private (but recorded) comments he has been banned from attending any NBA events. He will have to pay a $2.5 million fine. The NBA is trying to force him to sell his property (L.A. Clippers).

While his comments were offensive and disgusting (and he is obviously an elitist prick), should anyone be able to ban him from public events or force him to pay a fine or sell his property for something he said in a private conversation?

Almost as soon as this story broke the race baiter Al Sharpton was threatening to call for an advertising boycott of the NBA during an interview with TMZ if Sterling is not punished for his speech.

And who could forget the Paula Dean fiasco where while under oath during a court appearance she admitted to using the dreaded "N-word" in a private conversation with her husband in the past? As a result, she was fired from the Food Network and was dropped by sponsors. Her merchandise was pulled from store shelves across the nation. All because of something she said 20 years ago in a private conversation with her husband.

The list could go on and on. But I do not want to waste any more time on this. The race issue is being constantly poked by operatives of the federal government like Al Sharpton to keep racial tensions high. The government controlled mainstream media uses this racial tension as a distraction to keep everyone occupied. The infighting serves as a distraction so we don't come together and so we don't see what is really happening with their corruption and attacks on out freedom.

They want to keep us divided along racial lines so that they can better lie to and control us.

An Entitlement Mentality

Sadly, the United States is turning from being a nation of producers to a nation of takers. Far too many feel that they are entitled to "free money" for doing nothing.

According to http://www.heritage.org/

> America is increasingly moving away from being a nation of self-reliant individuals, where civil society flourishes, toward being a nation of individuals less inclined to practicing self-reliance and personal responsibility. Government programs not only crowd out civil society but too frequently trap individuals and families in long-term dependence, leaving them incapable of escaping their condition for generations to come.

And according to Statistic Brain http://goo.gl/s0AXYH as of July 8th, 2014, there were 12,800,000 Americans on welfare, 46,700,000 on food stamps or SNAP, 5,600,000 on unemployment, with a total government spending on welfare annually (not including food stamps or unemployment) of $131.9 billion. Folks these are the true zombies. These are the people who will be clawing at your door when the federal government collapses and the welfare handouts stop coming.

Foreign Companies Taking Over Big Business and Buying up Property in The U.S.

China and to a lesser extent other nations are buying up business and property in the United States. For example, China recently purchased 90% ownership in AIG's airplane leasing unit http://goo.gl/BTMjza, International Lease Finance Corporation. It was purchased by a Chinese investor group for approximately

16

$5.28 billion. And according to the same site the Chinese have bought 80.1 percent of ILFC for approximately $4.23 billion, with an option for an additional 9.9 percent stake. According to its website, ILFC is 'world's largest independent aircraft lessor measured by number of owned aircraft.'

And it's not only airplanes that the Chinese are interested in. CNBC reports http://goo.gl/KXVe2N that the Chinese are on a buying spree and sweeping up every energy and natural resource in the United States that they can get their hands on. In addition, they are even buying up and taking control of the U.S. food supply. China's largest acquisition to date of the U.S. company, Smithfield Foods. There are market watchers who question China's interest in taking possession of one of America's largest food producers.

And they're not stopping there. The Chinese are also buying large chunks of land across America, according to Michael Snyder of the Economic Collapse Report http://goo.gl/aUCe6D. The Chinese are on a real estate buying spree all over America.

"Wrongheaded" Americans Must Trust Government More

President Obama recently said that Americans have developed the "wrongheaded" view that Washington will not look out for them, a fallacy he said that has been stoked by conservatives and their mistrust of the federal government.

If you disagree with Al Gore and others on global warming then you probably have a psychiatric disorder http://goo.gl/rNA4vd. If you don't want to join the Borg, then you undoubtedly have a psychiatric disorder. Psychiatrists now say non-conformity is a mental illness http://goo.gl/2zckMK. Yep, nothing to see here folks, take your meds and relax. Everything is going to be okay. No more "wrongheaded" Americans allowed. You will be assimilated into the collective http://goo.gl/ZzGBTU.

This is being done for a couple of reasons. Number one if the government can legally declare you a nutcase (for whatever reason they come up with), then they can legally take away your rights or lock you up. No one wants to be labeled or considered a crazy person, so most folks will shut-up and keep their thoughts about the government and governmental policy to themselves. And that is the purpose.

U.S. National Debt at Unprecedented Levels

As of May 13 2014, the current national debt stands at 17,518,681,450,890. Yep, that is a lot of numbers. Over seventeen trillion in debt and growing fast. To put it into perspective and to see what a trillion dollars looks like see demonocracy.info/infographics/usa/us_debt/us_debt.html.

How much longer this spending and adding to the national debt can go on before completely crashing is up for debate but the world is starting to lose faith in the U.S. dollar and is looking to move away from and out of the U.S. currency.

When the world (or a couple of key countries) lose faith in or dump the U.S. dollar and stop lending to us (because of our massive growing debt and our out of control currency printing), the U.S. economy will crash. This will not happen overnight. It has been happening for years. As we get closer to "the end" the whole process will be put into overdrive. We can see this starting now with our lenders using their dollars to buy euros or yen, or buying gold rather than U.S. bonds.

The U.S. dollar is backed by nothing but air and everyone with half a brain knows it. The fact that many people still view the U.S. dollar as having some value allows you to be able to make purchases with it. The dollar is continually decreasing in buying power and will continue to do so until it approaches zero worth.

This continued decrease in value is caused mostly by the continued and uncontrolled currency printing and the increasing national debt. For a complete breakdown of how the financial system "works" and how it will collapse please read Dollar Collapse FAQ's http://goo.gl/6Vjzi3. This is by far the best and easiest to understand the explanation that I've found.

I could go on forever and we could get into issues like our failed foreign policy, the three global predator nations all fighting for control and to be the leader of the new world order, the corrupt banking system, the vulnerable power grid, pandemic disease etc. but we will leave that for another day.

And is that is why I am a prepper.

Chapter 2

WATER: DRINK OR DIE

Without the threat of severe weather or the need for immediate emergency medical care, potable water will be your first concern following any type of disaster. I always advise my consulting clients to strive for at least three independent sources of water for cooking and drinking. For example, stored water, a water well and rainwater collection system.

I cannot stress the need for reliable water sources enough. Without water, most people will die in only 3-4 days--a lot sooner if the weather is hot and you have no shelter, or you have to do a lot of physical labor or activity. A person needs about two quarts of water per day to stay healthy barring extreme weather or a lot of physical exertion.

Adding a minimum of one gallon of water for cooking, cleaning, and sanitation, a medium sized family of four would need almost 30 gallons of water per week, minimum just to stay alive. That is around 900 gallons per year. Unfortunately, most preppers do not have enough room to store 900 gallons of water. Therefore, I suggest you strive for at a minimum 55 gallons per person. If you live in an arid region of the country, I suggest you double or triple this amount.

You will also need to have several different methods of water purification available to you. We will go into detail about water purification methods in the following paragraphs, as well as how to store water long-term.

A Death by Contaminated Water: A few years ago, my grandfather told me a story that illustrates how deadly contaminated water can be. It happened in the summer of 1934 when he was only 9 years old. He was out in the fields gathering corn with his dad, brothers, and sister. He said it had to be at least 100 degrees because the sun was bright in the sky and the sweat burned his eyes as it dripped from his forehead.

His eleven-year-old sister got thirsty and instead of going to the house to get water, she drank from a nearby stream. She died a few days later. Upon further investigation, it was discovered that a cow from a nearby farm had died upstream from where she drank, contaminating the water.

They had used the water from this spot for years with no ill effects. They thought it was safe but it was not, at least not at that point in time.

From U.S. Army Field Manual 21-76

By drinking non-potable water, you may contract diseases or swallow organisms that can harm you. Examples of such diseases or organisms are:

- Dysentery - Severe, prolonged diarrhea with bloody stools, fever, and weakness.
- Cholera and typhoid - You may be susceptible to these diseases regardless of inoculations.
- Flukes - Stagnant, polluted water--especially in tropical areas--often contains blood flukes. If you swallow flukes, they will bore into the bloodstream, live as parasites, and cause disease.
- Leeches - If you swallow a leech, it can hook onto the throat passage or inside the nose. It will suck blood, create a wound, and move to another area. Each bleeding wound may become infected.

Moreover, pollutants from human activities often find their way into the water—e.g., trash, animal feces, fertilizers, herbicides, oils, heavy metals, salts and pollutants from vehicles etc. It's impossible to tell with 100% certainty what water is safe to drink without laboratory testing.

There are, however, some general guidelines that can help. Running water is generally safer than still water. Below are tips to keep in mind as you look for water:

- Look for clear water.
- Avoid water that has algae growing in it.
- Avoid discolored water.
- Avoid water from marshes/swamps.
- Avoid cloudy water.
- Avoid water that has an odor.
- Avoid floodwater.
- Water always flows downhill.
- Listen for the sound of frogs.
- Never eat snow without first melting it to avoid speeding up hypothermia.
- Freshly fallen snow on a clean surface is fine but old snow might be contaminated with bacteria.
- Never drink water from a lake or stream that is near or downstream from agricultural land, factories or mines.
- Rainwater is perfectly drinkable as it falls from the sky.
- The safest way to treat questionable water is to first boil it and then filter it.

Berkey Water Filters

The spring water where I live runs in a constant flow from the side of the mountain and it is as clear as bottled water; however, I will not drink it or use it for cooking without first running it through my Berkey water filter. A good water filter is necessary and one of the very first survival preps that you should invest in. I suggest that your first choice is a Berkey water filter system.

My dad and grandfather drive out to my place most weekends and fill their jugs from the spring – they drink and cook using the water without any filtration or other purification. They have never had any trouble. Still, I prefer to filter all of my water before drinking.

The Berkey filters are extremely effective at removing pathogenic bacteria, cysts, parasites, chemical contaminants and impurities. The elements have an indefinite shelf life and will filter at least 3,000 gallons of water before needing replacement. My filters are stored in zip-lock bags inside a small plastic tote.

Making an Improvised Water Filter

You can also make an improvised water filter as illustrated in the images below. Although this filter is not as effective as commercially available filters such as the Berkey, it beats no filtration at all and is easy to make using commonly available materials.

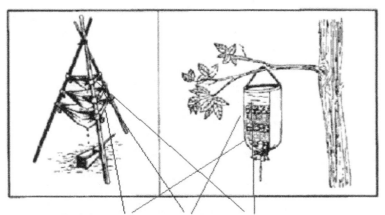

Layered with Charcoal, Sand and Gravel.

Boiling Water

Boiling water is one of the surest methods of water purification. This method of water purification will effectively kill viruses and bacteria. However, boiling will not remove chemicals and other pollutants such as lead, oil, and fuel.

To purify water by boiling all you need is a heat source, a suitable container, and water. Bring the water to a rolling boil to kill any viruses or bacteria that may be present. Contrary to what a lot of survival "experts" say, you do not have to boil the water for five to ten minutes in order to kill any viruses and bacteria that it might be harboring. All that is required is that the water reaches a rolling boil.

Warning: boiled water tastes stale; however, the taste is improved greatly by pouring the water back and forth between two containers to re-oxygenate it.

Sodis Method of Water Purification

The Sodis method of water purification is one of the simplest and most cost effective water purification methods available to the prepper or anyone needing potable water; however, like boiling, the Sodis water purification method does not remove chemicals, metals or other solids.

All you need is plastic bottles (PET) or glass, water and sunlight. The image below from https://goo.gl/m03zMY explains it better than I can in words (image used with permission).

Use clean PET bottles | Fill bottles with water, and close the cap | Expose bottles to direct sunlight for at least 6 hours (or for two days under very cloudy conditions) | Store water in the SODIS bottles | Drink SODIS water directly from the bottles, or from clean cups

Water Purification Tabs

Water purification tabs have been used by hikers and the military for years. They are a lightweight and portable way to effectively purify water for safe consumption. However, like boiling and the Sodis method above these tabs will not remove chemicals or metals.

The military suggests adding two tablets to a quart of water and letting it sit for thirty minutes or more before drinking. However, there are a number of different brands water purification tablets on the market and you should follow the exact instructions for the brand you are using.

Purification with Bleach

Water purification with bleach is one of those methods detailed in every survival book and any article that even hints at ways to purify water. However, it is not my first choice. If possible, I would use another method such as boiling or Sodis.

Water treated with bleach (only use unscented bleach to purify water) tastes like, well like bleach. Long-term use may lead to an increased cancer risk. I do not like it and will not use it unless no other alternative is available.

Add four drops of unscented bleach (or two teaspoons per ten gallons) to each two-liter of water and let stand for 30 minutes before using.

Making Urine Drinkable through Distillation

Urine can be made drinkable (and clean) via simple distillation, this will also work for seawater. However, the downside to distillation is that it takes a significant amount of energy, to boil the water for the duration required.

Pre-filtering

No matter what water purification method you are, using it is a good idea to "pre-filter" any dirty or murky water. You can use a coffee filter, a clean shirt, or a bandana. This will help remove any larger particles from the water, making it more potable and increasing the life of water filters used.

Water Storage

As for water storage, I have six five-gallon containers that I bought at Wal-Mart in the sporting goods department. I have also set up a 200-gallon rainwater catchment system and another 55-gallon food grade barrel that I installed to catch water runoff from the roof of my chicken coop. I use this water for my chickens, but of course, if needed, I could filter and drink it too.

If you live in one of the drier desert regions, water would be a major concern and that may necessitate the storage of thousands of gallons of water for an emergency.

A rainwater catchment can be as sophisticated as the one pictured below or as simple as purchasing a livestock watering tank or kiddie pool and catching the water from your downspouts or the rain as it falls. You can also rig up tarps or plastic sheeting to funnel the rain water into the container.

Do not store water in used five-gallon milk jugs. They are not strong enough for long-term storage and eventually will break down and leak. The five-gallon containers sold in the sporting goods section of most department stores work great as do the 55-gallon food-grade plastic drums.

Just be sure the drums are clean and contained no harmful chemicals before filling. If you must use small containers, empty 2-liter soda bottles work well. They are stronger than the aforementioned milk jugs and have better lids and are more convenient to use.

A Note about Tap Water for Long-Term Storage

If you are storing tap water from a municipal water system, there is usually no need to add bleach as suggested by some writers. Water from the municipal tap already contains enough chlorine to prevent any bacterial growth and can be stored without any other additives.

When putting water away for long-term storage, I use a Water Preserver Concentrate from Amazon.com instead of bleach. Water preserver concentrate will extend the storage life to up to five years.

Choosing the Right Retreat Property to Ensure Water Independence

When buying a retreat property, your first consideration should be to secure a reliable, non-grid dependent water source. The best source would be a deep well (have it tested before using, especially if it's an old well). The next best option would be a full-time spring. The next best option would be a river or creek, or even a pond or lake. All water from ponds, rivers, and streams should be treated as if it is contaminated with the worst pathogens, just to be on the safe side. Better safe than sorry, I always say.

Chapter 3
FOOD STORAGE

Storing enough food to survive unassisted and on your own for three to six months (or a full year or even longer) is the where most new preppers get overwhelmed and some even give up altogether. While I agree that storing and rotating such a large amount of food on a continual basis can be a lot of work and requires dedication, it is by no means impossible. If done right can even be fun.

But where do you start? You should start with the basics. Wheat (or other grains, for those who cannot tolerate wheat), rice, beans, oats, corn, salt, honey, cooking oil, powdered milk, canned fruits, vegetables, and meats are some of the least expensive foods you can buy. They store well and provide a balanced diet.

Generally, the most feasible plan is to store the foods that you normally eat on a daily basis. Start with one month of food and build your supply from there. This can be easier said than done, especially if you eat the typical American from the drive-thru at the local fast food joint. If that is the case, then you need to change your diet.

By including your storage foods into your everyday meals you avoid the shock of a radical change in diet if forced to live off your food storage.

Wheat

This is the backbone of your survival diet. Wheat is nature's longest storing seed. It has an indefinite shelf life given proper storage conditions. Wheat (and other grains) can also be sprouted, adding fresh greens to the diet even in winter.

Rice

Rice is my favorite storage food and I actually prefer rice to wheat for storage. But that is a personal preference. White rice stores better and has a longer shelf life than brown rice; however, brown rice has more nutritional value. Despite the trade-off in storage duration, I still prefer brown rice for storage because of the added nutritional value.

Beans

Beans, corn and rice combined make a complete food, providing just about everything you need to survive. Add fresh green sprouts or garden produce. Add extra vitamin C just to be sure you are getting enough nutrients to avoid scurvy and you will be well fed and healthy.

I like to store a combination of pinto beans, black beans, and mung beans. How much you store of each will depend on your personal preferences.

Oats

Do not go overboard when storing oats. Approximately 20 pounds per adult per year is plenty. Oats have a storage life of approximately four to six years depending on storage conditions and whether they have been opened after being packaged for long-term storage.

Corn

Corn equals cornmeal, cornbread, cornmeal mush, corn cakes and a huge list of other foods that you can prepare using the seed. It is best to store whole corn because it stores much better and has, at least, double the shelf life of cracked corn.

Salt

While not a food but a mineral, salt is nonetheless essential to the diet and individual health. Salt is also used in the preservation of food and animal products. Salt, like wheat, has an indefinite shelf life. Store at least 10 pounds of iodized salt per person, per year.

It is also a good idea to stock up on salt blocks to attract game animals for future harvesting. You can find these in the sporting goods stores and other outlets that sell to hunters. You can also get these through your local farmers' co-op where they sell them for domestic livestock supplementation.

Honey or Sugar

As a sweetener, honey makes an unequaled contribution to the diet. Honey, like wheat and salt, has an indefinite shelf life. Store at least 10 pounds per person. If the honey hardens and crystallizes, heat it slowly in a double boiler to reconstitute.

Cooking Oil

There is some controversy as to which is best for storage in the prepper's pantry, vegetable oil, or olive oil. Both will work fine. You should stock up on the one that you like best. I recommend putting away 10 quarts per person, per year.

Powdered Milk

Most people turn their nose at the thought of powdered milk, preferring whole milk from the supermarket. Granted it does have a slightly different taste, but it is not unpleasant to drink and after a week or two, it seems to "grow" on you. Studies have shown that nonfat powdered milk has a storage life of 20 years or more when packaged (nitrogen-packed) and stored properly.

Stockpiling Hard To Store Foods

I prefer to buy those hard-to-store long-term items like powdered milk, dry margarine, butter powder, buttermilk powder, cheese powder; shortening and powdered eggs prepackaged for long-term storage in #10 metal cans from Augason Farms or other reputable survival food vendors.

If packaged and stored correctly, powdered milk stores fairly well and will last for several years; however, powdered milk is one of the most difficult food products to store long-term.

Light, moisture, and oxygen all cause the milk powder to degrade quickly. When properly stored using Mylar bags, oxygen absorbers and desiccants inside five-gallon buckets shelf life can be extended greatly.

Plastic buckets are slightly porous. As such, a minute amount of air will permeate the contents of the bucket. However, by correctly packing and sealing the product in Mylar bags the exposure to oxygen can be significantly reduced.

The best way to ensure that you always have a fresh supply is to rotate it into your normal everyday meal plan and use products on a first in first out basis. This will ensure you do not have any problems. This is true for all of your other storage foods as well. Use it and replace it.

Please note to ensure maximum shelf life I buy most of my powdered milk stock commercially packaged from Augasonfarms.com or one of the other long-term storage food vendors.

Supermarket Canned Foods

Canned foods from the supermarket have many advantages when it comes to food storage. They have a decent shelf life--on average of 2-5 years for most products. (Note: shelf life means that the foods retain 100% of their listed original nutritional value up until that point. In most cases, store bought canned foods remain edible far past the listed expiration dates.)

As long as the cans are not bulging, rusted through or punctured and the foods smell fresh upon opening then I would not hesitate to eat canned goods that are far past their listed expiration date. However, that is a personal choice and one you will have to make yourself.

Store bought canned foods have several advantages over freeze-dried or dehydrated foods, including cost and calories per serving. Another advantage is that canned foods already contain water so there is no need to use any potable water from your storage to rehydrate them.

Despite the advantages of canned foods over freeze-dried and dehydrated foods, canned goods do have some disadvantages— e.g., weight, space needed for storage and shelf life.

I recommend a combination of the basic foods such as wheat, rice, and beans, store bought canned foods as well as certain "packaged for long-term storage" foods that are hard to store such as powdered milk.

All canned foods should be dated using a permanent marker and rotated on a FIFO (first-in-first-out) basis. I suggest that you build a rotating canned food shelf that will automatically rotate your canned foods when cans are added and pulled from the shelf. Plans can be found at http://goo.gl/KeQsWq

Always keep a notepad beside the shelf or in your kitchen and write down every item that you take from the shelf. Take the note with you on your next trip to the supermarket so you can buy and restock the items that you have taken from the shelf. That way you always have a fully stocked pantry and a fresh supply of food.

Don't Forget the Can Opener

Sure you could use a knife to open cans but a manual can opener is easier and safer. So whatever else you do, do not forget the can opener. I suggest that you buy several of the strongest made ones that you can find.

Other Foods

After you get the basic foods listed above in the needed proportions (see below), it is a simple matter to add other foods as you get the extra money.

*Canned meats: We all know that SPAM is the preppers go to for a cheap "meat" source that has a longer than average shelf life and a high fat content. Canned hams, tuna, salmon, chicken, and turkey are all welcome additions to any pantry. Stock-up on the meats that your family normally eats. Date and rotate just as you would any other canned food.

*White flour: White flour from the store has a much longer shelf life than whole wheat flour because it has been "processed" to remove the oily germ. Unfortunately, this "processing" also removes much of the nutritional value of the flour.

Processed white flour has a shelf life of over five years if kept dry and safe from pests (like the meal moth). Mill moths get into the flour, lay eggs and those eggs turn into flour weevils, which spoil the flour. Look for tiny dark specks in the flour, as this is the first sign that the flour is infested.

If it clumps together because of settling just break it apart and run it through a sifter before use.

Store flour for long-term storage in airtight containers with oxygen absorbers. See details below. You can also freeze flour before you put into five-gallon buckets. Freezing will kill any meal moths that happen to have been trapped inside before they can do any damage to the flour.

Most of my "flour" is in the form of whole-wheat berries that I have to mill (grind) before use. However, I do have some processed flour in my pantry for lazy days when I do not feel like grinding whole wheat into usable flour.

*Peanut butter: Peanut butter is a good source of protein, fat, and calories and has a decent shelf life. Peanut butter is also an energy food and one that I always take on hunting and camping trips. Unopened peanut butter will last for years.

*Spices: Be sure to include a good selection of spices in your food storage. Spices can make even the most repugnant foods palatable and can help to alleviate food boredom. Cinnamon, turmeric, paprika, ginger, oregano, and garlic are some my favorites and that make up the bulk of the spices in my pantry.

*Baking powder, baking soda, and yeast: Baking powder, baking soda, and yeast (keep yeast frozen to extend shelf life) are also essential since you are storing and baking with unprocessed grains.

*Dried pasta: Dried pasta will keep indefinitely if kept dry in bug and rodent proof containers.

Comfort Foods

Storing a sufficient amount of "comfort foods" is very important to your psychological well-being as well as to alleviate food boredom that is sure to set in after eating only storage foods for several months. Comfort foods are even more important if you have children or need to care for the elderly.

Consider comfort foods such as Jell-O, instant pudding mixes, cake mixes, hard candies, chewing gum, Spaghettios, mac and cheese, brownie mixes, canned spaghetti and meatballs, mashed potatoes, popcorn, cocoa, tea, coffee, powdered juice mixes, sunflower seeds, etc. In addition, remember to date and rotate on a FIFO basis.

We crave variety and having a supply of familiar comfort foods can go a long way toward retaining our sanity and positive outlook during a long-term disaster. You can only deny yourself for so long before desperation and depression will overwhelm. Life will be difficult enough; give yourself a treat. You deserve it.

It is a fact that if forced to eat foods we do not want or the same foods for extended periods just to stay alive dissociation begins to set in. We begin to float away as an escape. We still eat to stay alive but suffer a lack of focus and become disorientated in relation to our surroundings.

This is dangerous in a survival setting. Most people think "that won't happen to me". Try eating nothing but beans and rice for three months and you will get a new perspective. Having a supply of comfort foods can help by providing, at least, some form of normalcy in your life.

Older folks and children will have the hardest time adjusting to new or unfamiliar foods with many refusing to eat altogether, especially if the food is unnecessarily bland or unappetizing. Comfort foods will help them cope.

Using Coupons to Save Money When Stockpiling Your Pantry

Using coupons offers an opportunity for huge saving on your preps that you should be taking advantage of. According to Wikipedia.com, a coupon is "A ticket or document that can be exchanged for a financial discount or rebate when purchasing a product. Coupons first saw widespread use in the United States in 1909 when Post conceived the idea to help sell their breakfast cereals". The concept is nothing new.

When I was in my early teens, I remember my mother clipping coupons from the Sunday paper; she would organize them in a small purse that she kept just for the purpose. She would wait for double or triple coupon deals to be advertised and then she would go shopping.

I remember one time she managed to get over $260 worth of stuff for less than $10. I was impressed.

I have used coupons to save money and stock up on survival supplies for several years and the saving can really add up fast. I have used coupons to save when buying everything from canned foods and tissue paper to toothpaste and dog food.

Now with the age of the internet, there is no need to clip coupons from the Sunday paper. You can easily find discounts for virtually any product by simply going online and printing them off with your home printer. Two of my favorite places for this is Coupons.com and MyPoints.com.

Using coupons may not exhibit the typically perceived image of a survivalist but it sure makes a lot of sense from a financial standpoint.

I think the main reason many people avoid using coupons is that they are afraid of looking poor (even if they are). This is nonsense and, really, who gives a rat's about what the person waiting in line behind you thinks. I do not. If they do not like it they're free to move over to the next checkout lane.

Stop worrying about what other people think. Trust me your life will be better when you do.

Before you can start using coupons to save on your survival supplies you will obviously need coupons. Coupons are all over the place you just have known where to look.

The bulk of mine are printed off from the web or clipped from the Sunday newspaper. I have worked out a deal with a local store owner where I get the papers they do not sell for free. I often get ten or more all loaded with coupon inserts.

The vendor only has to send the header of the papers that didn't sell back to the publisher to get credit for unsold papers; the newspaper doesn't want the old papers back and could care less what the vendor does with them.

If you do not want to buy the local paper and getting a local vendor to give you the leftover papers is not an option, you can often get the paper and the coupons free by asking friends, neighbors, and relatives who buy the paper to pass it on to you when they are done reading it.

It is common knowledge among coupons users that some of the best coupons are found in print magazines, coupon mailers, food packaging inserts, and grocery store receipts.

Once you start clipping and using coupons, you will need to a way to stay organized. You will need to be able to find what you are looking when you need it, and to know what you have so you can avoid letting your coupons expire without using them.

I use a recipe box with dividers and sort by date and coupon type. For example, I will sort under labels such as canned foods, deserts, over the counter meds, canned beans, rice and oats, dog food, kitchen supplies, etc.

Working out a system to stay organized is not difficult but it will go a long way toward maximizing savings and reducing your frustration. You can buy ready-made coupon organizers but I prefer my box because it was free. I go through my coupons once a month and weed out coupons that have expired or that I no longer want to use.

When using coupons, you will be tempted to buy stuff that you really do not need or never intended to buy just because you have a coupon for it. Do not do it. Unless of course you can get it free. If you start buying stuff you do not need just because you have a coupon you will then end up losing money.

Be sure to check prices before you make any purchases. Keep in mind that even with coupons, some brand named products cost more than the store brand, even when using coupons. Never buy a more expensive product because it has a brand name on it. Many of these store brands are from the same manufacturers as the store brands.

Watch for sales and stock up on items that you use that are on sale, especially when you have coupons for those items. Remember some stores offer "Double Coupon Sales" or even "Triple Coupon Sales" that actually doubles the value of the coupons you have. Such offers can lead to huge savings on the items you need.

In addition, do not overlook rebates and refund opportunities that are sometimes offered by product manufacturers. Most manufacturers require you buy the product and then mail in the cash register receipt along with the UPC bar code from the product. Keep these organized and send for the rebate or refund ASAP so you do not forget and possibly let the offer expiration date pass.

Vitamins

To ensure that you are getting a sufficient amount of needed daily vitamins and minerals for optimum health, you need to stockpile a good multi-vitamin and mineral supplement. Also consider extra vitamin C and vitamin D. Vitamin D is of extra importance if you're forced to stay inside (bugging in) for a longer than normal period of time and thus are unable to receive the needed vitamin D producing sunlight that is required for optimal health.

Don't Forget about Your Pets

Do not forget to include a sufficient amount of food in your stockpile to feed your pets. A well-trained dog will increase your chances of survival because he or she can hunt and alert you to trespassers and other trouble. I prefer smaller dual-purpose breeds with my choice for a working dog being the Jack Russell terrier.

A Sample Three-Month Food Supply for One Adult

Wheat	75 Pound
Grains, rice, oats etc.	25 Pound
Canned meats	5 Pound
Canned margarine, powdered eggs etc.	2 Pound
Dried beans, peas, lentils, etc.,	6 Pound
Dried fruit juice and concentrates	6 Pound
Dried fruits or canned	25 Pound (if dried, then equal to this fresh weight

Comfort foods	3 Pound
Non-fat dried milk	25 pound
Peanut butter or substitute protein / fat source	3 pound
Dried potatoes	12 pound (equal to this fresh weight)
Salt	2 pound
Shortening oils	3 quarts
Sugar or honey	12 pound
Canned or dried vegetables	9 pound (if dried, then equal to this fresh weight)

Please bear in mind that the above list is only a sample to help you get started, the most useful food storage list is the one that you put together yourself. After all, who knows better than you do what you and your family like to eat and in what amounts?

Where to Put All this Food

After reading the above recommendations, you are probably asking yourself where in the heck you are going to store all of this food. Well, that is a good question and one that you alone can answer for your situation. Nonetheless, I will make a few suggestions that I hope will point you in the right direction.

The absolute best place is an underground bunker, root cellar, or basement. Unfortunately, most people do not have any of those and have to make due with other less ideal storage options. Consider a spare bedroom, attached garage, a detached storage building on your property or as a last-resort a nearby storage unit rental.

If possible put in an underground storage area of some sort to keep you storage foods safe (and you) safe from weather extremes as well as the main enemy of your food storage shelf life and that is heat. An excellent option (and inexpensive when compared to other suitable alternatives) is the buried shipping container.

How to Store Dried Beans and Grains at Home for Long-Term Storage with Oxygen Absorbers & Mylar Bags

I store all my grains, beans and other dry foods (besides sugar, salt, or sprouting seeds) inside food-grade five-gallon plastic buckets. There is some controversy over what is and is not food grade. Most (but not all) buckets with #2 inside a small triangle on the bottom are food-grade the only way to be reasonably certain is to contact the manufacturer and ask.

I buy mine from the local hardware store in the paint department. They also have them at my Wal-Mart, but I prefer to buy from local business owners if possible. Sometimes they can even be gotten free from bakeries and restaurants just make sure they only contained food products, not paint, chemicals, or other things that can make you sick or dead.

Foods packed in oxygen do not store as well as those in an oxygen free atmosphere. Oxygen absorbers (available from Emergency Essentials ®) work by removing the air from the enclosed container, leaving an atmosphere of 99% pure nitrogen in a partial vacuum inside the buckets.

Do not open the bag of oxygen absorbers until ready to use because they will absorb oxygen from the surrounding environment, rendering them useless. Have everything ready to go before you open the package. Any unused oxygen absorbers can be stored inside a small canning jar until needed.

Be sure to have everything ready to go before you start. Line the inside of the bucket with an appropriately sized Mylar bag (also available from Emergency Essentials ®) these help to keep light and moisture out, thereby extending the storage life of the foods inside.

The Mylar bag also offers a layer of protection between the food and the plastic bucket, if for some reason the bucket that you are using is not food-grade.

Pour the food into the buckets a little at a time, shaking each bucket as it is being filled to settle and distribute the contents. Fill each bucket to about ½ inch from the top and throw in one 2000 cc oxygen absorber in each five-gallon bucket of food.

Sealing the Mylar bag is simple. First roll the top of the bag closed on one end leaving an opening at the other. Then press out any air that trapped inside. Next place a 2x4 across the top of the bucket, pull the Mylar bag over the 2x4 and seal with a clothing iron set at the highest setting in a typical ironing fashion across the board.

Quickly put the lids on each bucket and pound shut by laying the board across the top and striking with a hammer or rubber mallet. After a few hours, the absorbers will create a vacuum that will cause the lids on the buckets to "pop down" indicating a good seal and a proper atmosphere for long-term storage. Be sure to label each with date, content, and weight, written on the front with a permanent marker.

Chapter 4

TOOLS FOR COOKING AND PROCESSING YOUR FOOD STORAGE

Most homes will already have most of what you will need to process and cook the foods from your survival pantry, items such as pots, pans, and other common household kitchen utensils. So we will not get into that. What we will cover are tools that most typical kitchens do not have on hand but that are necessary for the prepper's kitchen. So let us get started.

Choosing a Grain Mill

You need a grain mill now. Don't put it off another day. Even one of the least expensive models would be better than not having one at all. I know many of you want the best and that is great. Get the best if you can afford it. Just do not put it off any longer. Get a mill now.

If you cannot afford one of the better models, get a cheaper one; buy two or three of the cheaper models--that way if one breaks and cannot be repaired, you will still have spares to fall back on.

This goes along with my philosophy of the rule of three. Always have at least three independent sources of any survival necessity. Never put all your eggs in one basket. Too many things can happen to leave you with nothing, which is what we are trying to avoid by prepping in the first place.

While I cannot give recommendations on all the models currently available today (because I have not owned or used them all), I can tell you what I have and my thoughts on these which should, at least, get you started in the right direction.

I currently own four different grain mills, The Wonder Junior Deluxe Grain Mill, a Corona Landers, a Back to Basics and a Grizzly H7775.

Wonder Junior Deluxe Grain Mill

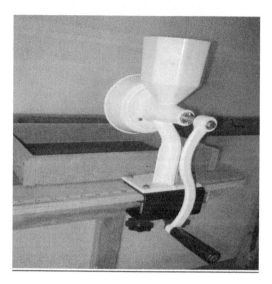

If you have read my book "Dirt Cheap Survival Retreat" you already know, that I used the Corona hand grain mill for all of my day-to-day milling. It is a strong and well-built grain mill and for less than $75, it is hard to beat.

The Mill to Table Clamping System is a Very Strong Feature
Included with the Wonder Mill

However, I have never liked having to run the meal through the Corona several times to produce usable fine enough flour for baking. That is one reason I made my homemade sifter was to speed up the process. However, it was still always necessary to run the bulk of the flour through the mill two or more times.

Since I mill grain several times per week I needed a more efficient mill. I considered the Country Living Grain Mill but never could find enough extra change for the purchase. Therefore, I started looking for an alternative. I eventually decided to order the Wonder Mill Deluxe from www.thewondermill.com.

I have used the Wonder Mill for the past three weeks and so far, I have been extremely pleased with my new mill. In fact, I think I have retired the Corona and will be using the wonder mill deluxe exclusively. Yeah, it is that good.

The Wonder Mill comes with both stone and steel grinding heads as shown in the photo above.

I love the one-piece construction of the mill and hopper. There is no separate hopper that can fall off during operation or any pins or clamps that could be lost. This is one thing I never liked about the Corona, as there were several times the hopper fell off during aggressive cranking of the handle.

Another big improvement over most hand operated grain mills is the double clamping system used on the Wonder Mill, which is the strongest I have ever seen on any mill. When properly clamped to the table, I had no problems with the mill moving out-of-place or coming off during grinding.

However, since all of my grinding is done in the same place, I will likely remove the clamp altogether and bolt the Wonder Mill directly to the table. This will provide the strongest possible mill to table mounting system.

Another thing I loved about the Wonder Mill is the quick change head system that allows you to easily switch from grinding dry grains, beans, and legumes to oily grains, nuts and even coffee in just a couple of minutes. The Wonder Mill Deluxe comes with both steel and stone grinding heads, which can be changed out in less than one minute.

Here are the product specifications:

- Weight: 10 pounds
- Height: 12 ¾ inches (without clamp)
- Hopper capacity: one quart
- Crank handle: 10 inches

Best of all, the Wonder Mill produces excellent, fine flour (with no sifting or re-grinding required). This saves a lot of time and effort. Moreover, the consistency is easily adjusted using a simple knob to adjust from pastry flour to cracked grains.

In fact, 90% of flour files through the sifter screen after the first pass through the mill. Again, this is a huge improvement over the Corona. In addition, because of the excellent bearing system (that never needs lubricating) cranking the handle is much smoother, but still requires effort.

The flour guide directs the falling flour into the catch pan or onto the screen without any mess around the milling heads or thrown flour on the table and floor. This is always been a problem with the Corona when grinding pieces of grain and flour would be thrown all over the place. One solution was to secure a plastic bag over the grinding head of the Corona to catch the flour and grain particles.

I wish that I had a Country Living Mill to compare against the Wonder Mill. I am sure there would have been some interesting findings with the comparison. The folks at WonderMill.com did perform a speed comparison between the two and according to their website:

In a test performed at the Wonder Mill test kitchen, the Wonder Junior was able to grind 1 ¼ cups of flour in a single minute *80 turns* (see our video speed test). This is 65% (about 1/2 cup) more than we were able to produce with the Country Living grain mill with the same flour setting and the same amount of turns *80 turns*, and for half the price.

I know what you are thinking, it sounds great but "can it be motorized"? Yes, it can. There is a motoring pulley available that will allow you to do just that; however doing so will void the warranty. They also make a special adapter which can be used with a power drill to make grinding any grains or beans a quick and easy process.

I only grind a small amount of flour at a time. (Why grind more than I need?) I will not be adding a motor but it is an option to keep in mind.

Your next question is probably going to be "what will it grind"? I have used it to grind wheat, corn, and beans. It can also grind spices, herbs, oily grains, nuts, and seeds. See WillItGrind.com for more info on what the Wonder Mill will grind.

Based on my tests, comparisons, price, and use, I give the Wonder Junior Hand Grain Mill my highest recommendation for a grain mill. If you are looking for a hand grain mill this is the one you should get.

Corona Landers Mill

The Corona Landers Mill is shown in the photo above mounted to a table and ready for use.

It is strong, robust, well made and my second favorite grain mill. The Corona is a hand-cranked unit that uses rotating steel burrs to crack and grind corn, beans, grains, nuts, and seeds.

It is manufactured using cast-iron parts with an electro-tinned finish to guarantee a rustproof and easy to clean tool. I give it my second highest recommendation following the wonder junior hand grain mill.

Back To Basics Mill

This mill works well and is actually very easy to use. My main complaint is the small hopper that needs to be refilled after a few cranks of the handle. It is lightweight when compared to the Corona and I do not think it would stand up as well to continued usage.

Grizzly H7775 Mill

The Grizzly H7775 mill it is not my first choice but it sure beats having nothing at all. It sits low on the table, low enough that getting a large enough bowl under the head to catch the flour is difficult. I have this same problem when using the Corona. This is the main reason I use a homemade sifter to catch the grindings.

My other complaint is the small hopper, refilling it every few cranks can be an annoyance, at least for me. On the plus side, the grinder is efficient and the grinding plates are easily adjusted to the desired consistency.

While this is a good mill it is not of the quality of the Corona but note that it is half the price so buying two or more is an option.

Country Living Mill

While I do not own one of these mills, they are given the highest recommendations by those that do. A recent advertisement proclaims:

> The Country Living Grain Mill is one of the highest quality grain mills ever made. You could drop it on the floor, and it would likely hurt the floor more than the grain mill. The Country Living Grain Mill is one of those high-quality items that could be passed on to the next generation.

51

How to Grind Grains and Beans

When grinding it is often necessary to regrind the grain several times before reaching the desired consistency. Some of the meal will come out perfectly fine the first time through while other parts remain coarse and need to be reground several times.

One way to make grinding easier is to use a screen to sift out the finer flour while leaving the larger pieces of grain behind. The sifter is simply a four-sided box with sides but no top and a bottom made of nylon window screen from the hardware store. Mine is 15" X 12" with sides made of a ¾ inch by 3-1/2 wood.

A homemade flour sifter screen is shown in the photo above.

Cut the wood to length, and nail or screw the pieces together. Lay the screen out on a hard surface, sit the box down flat on top of the screen, and cut to fit with a utility knife. Turn the box over and tack the screen to the box with several thumbtacks or small nails to hold the screen in place.

Take all-purpose cement from the plumbing department of the hardware store, and spread generously around the rim of the box over the edge of the screen, forming a permanent seal between the wood and the screen.

When grinding, place a section of newspaper under the grinder head and set the box on top. Grind as normal but after each pass through the grinder, shake the finer meal onto the newspaper and transfer into a bowl.

Pour the coarser meal back into the grinder and regrind, repeating until reaching the desired constancy. This saves running the finer meal back through the mill, making grinding easier and quicker.

How to Clean Field Run Wheat

First off, never buy "seed" grain for human consumption. Seed grain is often treated with insecticides and fungicides. Seed grain is to be planted and grown not eaten. Buy untreated whole grain sold as "feed" that is meant to be eaten.

Look for "field run grain." It is cheaper and because of fewer processing steps, it is less likely to be infected with mold or contaminated. Field run wheat will have dirt and detritus that will need to be removed before use but cleaning wheat is not a big deal.

First, sort the grain by laying it out on a clean surface and pick out any chunks of dirt, rocks or darker grain. After sorting, you need to wash the grain. Place the grain on a sifter or screen and pour clean water over it until the water coming out the bottom is as clean as that poured in from the top.

After cleaning the grain, you will need to dry it before grinding. Pour the grain into a strainer and set it aside for about ten minutes. After it stops dripping spread it out on a cookie sheet about ¼ inch deep, heat in oven at 180° degrees occasionally stirring until dry. Drying usually takes about an hour. If it takes longer that's fine; just make sure it does not burn.

Alternatively, if you prefer you can dry it outside under the sun. This is better and cheaper but is dependent on the weather and time of day and the season. Just spread the grain out in a thin layer on newspaper or other suitable material in direct sunlight. A solar oven could also be used; however, I have never tried this method myself.

Cooking Tools and Related Items

Listed below are some of the best cooking stoves and related tools for preppers. I have all of these and they are all well-made and useful; however, it should be noted that you do not need to go out and buy one of each type of cooking stove. Get what is best for you in your location. For example, if you're located far north and don't get all that much sunshine, then you're probably better off skipping the solar oven and purchasing an EcoZoom rocket stove.

Zoom Versa Stove

The EcoZoom rocket stove is designed to burn wood, dried biomass (plant materials and animal waste used as fuel) or charcoal making it a truly versatile means of cooking now, especially after the lights go out and other more conventional sources of fuel (like propane) are no longer available or are in short supply.

My EcoZoom rocket stove has proven to be very heat efficient. It will bring a pan of water to a rolling boil in less than two minutes and frying an egg like nobody's business. Having a means of cooking when the power goes out should be self-explanatory. Having a cooking source that uses easy to find, renewable fuel is an extra bonus.

Camping Stove

Having a standard camping type stove on hand for emergencies is one of those common sense things to do and most folks in the country already have one or two of these for camping purposes.

If you do not then go out and buy one now. A top-of-the-line model will put you back around $100 at current prices. In addition, do not forget to pick up some extra fuel canisters. Put back at least 24 one-pound canisters or better yet get a hook-up that will allow the use of the larger 20-pound tanks.

Sun Oven

If you are in an area that receives a sufficient amount of sunlight then a solar oven is must have. With a solar oven there is no need to store or scrounge for fuel and as long as the sun is hot in the sky you will have an unlimited "fuel" source to prepare food.

The best brand and the one that I recommend is The All American Sun Oven. It is best to get the package with the accessories included in order avoid having to buy these later.

Folding Camp Grill

A folding camp grill is another item like the camping stove above that most folks in the country already have on hand. But it is worth mentioning here. Every prepared prepper should have one of these. So if for some strange reason you do not then go get one as soon as possible.

I bought mine at Wal-Mart in the sporting goods department for under twenty-five dollars. They also have them at Amazon.com.

Volcano Collapsible Stove

Where the Volcano Stove is most useful is as an emergency cooking source at home or bug out location. With the ability to use several different fuel sources (wood, charcoal, or propane) it is versatile and well suited for the needs of preppers.

Another great thing about this stove is that it is not one of those products that you buy and then put away for the when the poop hits the fan; it can be used for everyday cooking or on weekends while grilling at the park with family.

Outdoor Grill / Smoker

This is another one of those items that will make like much easier at least when it comes to preparing food after a disaster or a long-term grid down situation. I bought mine at Wal-Mart in the lawn and garden department for less than one-hundred dollars. They also have them at Amazon.com.

Extra Large Stew Pot

Even if you don't anticipate having a large group to cook for you should still have at least one large stew pot because you never know who or how many family members or close friends will show up at your door and most of us don't want to shoot them so we will have to feed them. I have a Bayou Classic 7406, 6-Qt. Cast Iron Soup Pot with Cast Iron Lid but I am afraid that even this will not be sufficient for my needs.

Food Saver Vacuum Sealer

The Food Saver Series vacuum sealer is a great little machine that can greatly increase the shelf life of products. This is a highly recommended item for preppers!

Butchering Kit

Because most preppers are "knife collectors" of sorts, we often overlook the need for a good home butchering kit. Get the very best kit that you can afford. The Outdoor Edge Game Processor PR-1 12-Piece Portable Butcher Kit with Hard Side Carry Case is a good product for the price.

Chapter 5

ESSENTIAL SURVIVAL TOOLS AND GEAR

It seems everyone likes lists. Lists are a quick reference point and a guide when stockpiling survival gear. Keep in mind that this is only a guide and not a list formed in stone. The tools and gear that you include should be individualized for you and your needs.

After all, who knows your skills, location, and resources better than you do? However, with that being said, I feel this list is a good starting point and a thrust in the right direction. It represents the bare minimum amount of gear.

I have purposely left out such items as cookware, clothing, and other everyday household items. Every home should already have a plentiful supply of these everyday staples. I have also not included food, barter goods or firearms since these have already been or will be covered in more detail in other parts of this book.

I have tried to keep this list as short and as to the point as possible. I have included only items that I feel are essential. Sure, you could survive with less but with some basic gear, things become less of a challenge. If nothing else, it should generate discourse. Let us get started.

1. Water filter: Even though we talked about water and the Berkey filters earlier, it is such an important and vital piece of survival gear that it bears repeating. Get a good water filter. The one that I recommend is the Big Berkey filter system. You should also have a smaller portable filter for when you are on the move.
2. A Chainsaw: A chainsaw is essential if you are heating or planning to heat with wood. Even if you are not I still

recommend that you get one. A chainsaw can be used for a lot more than just cutting firewood. They can be used when building wooden structures, felling trees to blocking roads leading to your location.

3. Chainsaw Accessories: Now that you have a chainsaw you will need a few things to keep it running. To start, you will need mixing oil, bar/chain oil and files. A spare saw is also nice to have and the quickest "repair" when one saw goes down.

4. Basic Tool-Kit: Tools are essential prepper items and should not be overlooked. Instead of buying your tools one-at-a-time, it is quicker and in most cases cheaper to purchase a ready-made kit. After you have a basic kit, you can add tools as funds permit. Consider hand saws, drills, and other tools that do not require a source power to operate.

5. Electrical Generator: Current prices for electrical generators can range from just over one-hundred dollars to one thousand dollars or, even more, depending on what you get. I suggest that you get the best that you can afford. Consider purchasing a diesel-powered model over gasoline, if you can find and affordable one.

6. Work clothes and safety gear: Do not forget your safety when working with tools and saws. The last thing you need is to get hurt during a grid-down situation. Start by putting back at least 12 pairs of good quality work gloves and several pairs of steel-toed boots, as well as eye protection, protective chaps, hearing protection, etc. Always remember to work extra safe and to take every precaution to reduce the likelihood of getting hurt.

7. Five-gallon plastic buckets: it's a good idea to have several of these around; they have multiple uses—e.g., carrying water, animal feed, garden produce, tools, etc.

8. Hunting Deer & Game Hauler Cart: These carts work great for moving downed deer out of the woods. They also work great when moving heavy but awkward loads around the homestead. They will also work great on foraging trips after the crash where you need a way to haul scrounged supplies back to your survival retreat.

9. Plastic sheeting: Six-mill plastic sheeting has multiple uses from temporarily stopping a leaky roof, sealing the window, to improvised body bags. You should include at least one large roll in your preps.

10. Tools of your post-collapse trade: The best barter item is you and your skills, and you will need the necessary tools to apply your trade on hand and in good working order. I suggest that you include at least two of each of those tools without which it would be impossible to perform your trade.

11. Gardening Tools: Get the best tools that you can afford. Most of the "tools" sold at Wal-Mart are nothing but low-quality made-in-China junk that will fail under hard use and when you need them the most.

12. Reloading Gear: If you are not reloading your own ammo now, you need to start. I suggest that you buy a complete reloading kit to start instead of trying to put it all together one piece at a time.

13. Animal Traps: I prefer live traps and snares for survival food procurement purposes to leg-hold type traps. Leg-hold traps are designed for catching fur-bearing animals and are not as effective when it comes to catching meat for the stewpot.

14. Camp Toilet: We all have to go and we need a place to go, so I suggest that you have a camp toilet or a bucket with a screw on lid to hold human waste until you have time each day to dispose of it properly. In the country, build an

outhouse. Be sure to put back some hydrated lime--poop and then cover with a scoop of hydrated lime.

15. <u>Personal Items</u>: Get a quality sleeping bag and enough toilet paper, toothpaste, brushes, soap, tampons, eyeglasses, sunscreen, medications, birth control, etc. for each person in your group to last approximately one full year. This may be impossible with certain medications.

16. <u>Antibiotics:</u> Having a supply of antibiotics can mean the difference between life and death. For the survivor, unfortunately, laying in a good supply can be nearly impossible when going about it the traditional way. Fortunately, companies like Camping Survival are selling "fish antibiotics" that pharmacologically indistinguishable from those prescribed by your doctor. _Disclaimer:_ Always seek medical advice from a licensed professional for diagnoses and treatment options.

Chapter 6

THE BUG OUT BAG (aka BOB)

"Which is heavier a soldiers pack or a slaves chains" – Napoleon Bonaparte

There has been a lot of talk over the years about bugging out, bug out bags, and bug out bag lists. The subject of "bugging out" is bound to come up in any conversation about survival preps and every survival blog has, at least, one article posted about how to put together a bug out bag.

Why Bug Out?

The subject of bugging out and bug out bags (some preppers refer to this kit as a bug out backpack) is a popular one and for good reason. Disasters such as hurricanes, earthquakes, tornadoes, flash floods or another natural disaster could force survivors to "head for the hills" in search of safer ground.

We are constantly being threatened by potential disasters, both natural and manmade, such as war and economic collapse. It seems like we are being threatened from all sides and sometimes I admit to feeling like just throwing up my hands in despair and just giving up. It is easy to give up. Nevertheless, I shake it off and prep harder than before. I am funny like that.

We also face a series of potential long-term disasters including ecological collapse, economic collapse, agriculture disaster, war, plague, pandemic, an over oppressive government or any number of disasters that could force us to seek safer footing or even hide-out in the hills long-term.

Bugging Out Vs. Hunkering Down

If you have read my article bugging out vs. hunkering down at my website, then you already know that bugging out to the hills should be your last option when you have no other choice.

Bug out bags should be considered only as a temporary survival plan or as a backup at best. You should keep in mind that if you are forced to leave your home or retreat you have essentially made yourself a refugee, which is the last thing you want during hard times.

A bug out kit will keep you alive for a few days or weeks. What will you do after you supplies run out? You had better have a way to supply your basic needs after exhausting the gear contained in your bug out bag.

Keep in mind that we are not talking about bugging out from the city to a pre-set-up and well-stocked retreat in the hills. If this is your plan then you might not need a "bug out bag" since you can just load everything into your car and take off. However, having a bug out bag is still essential, i.e. life-saving gear in a pack or kit that is ready to grab and go is a good idea, particularly if you have to abandon your bug out vehicle and head out on foot.

It would be great if you already have a stockpile of food, medications, and gear waiting for you at a mountain retreat. Let us just hope that you can actually get past the blocked roads, carjackers, checkpoints, and other hazards that will be found along the way and get there unscathed.

If you do manage to make it through all of the hazards along the way to your well-stocked retreat in the hills, do not be surprised if you are "greeted" at the door by another family or group that has already moved in. What would you do? They may outnumber you and be better armed.

Will you walk away or stay and fight for what is yours?

If possible, move to your retreat or relocate to a safer area now, before disaster strikes. Learn to grow your own food, raise small livestock and get to know your neighbors. I just hope that it is not too late in the game for you to make the move. Time is running out and it may already be too late to relocate.

Anyways, back to bugging out and putting together a bug out bag.

Some survivalist aka "preppers" look at this type of bug out kit as an "escape and evasion" bag. Where they will use the kit as a grab and go bag that will be used if they are forced to head out to the forest or mountains to hide from danger. For most, this is a flawed idea.

Living completely free of civilization, scrounging for food and shelter in the forest, mountains, or desert for any significant length of time can be done under the right conditions by some people. However, it would not be easy. The constant struggle to stay alive would be more than many could handle and most would not make it very long.

But when you're left with no other option besides stay and die or bug out to the hills and maybe survive a few extra days, it's worth a try and having a "bug out or escape and evasion bag" ready to go will give you a better chance of making it.

The option of a hidden cave or dugout stocked with survival supplies should be a considered. Having a hidden cache of essential survival gear could mean the difference between death and survival if you are forced to head for the hills.

I have several cache tubes hidden around my area and have been working on putting in more. I will only leave my home/retreat if I have no other choice. I would rather stay and fight than run and hide. But if I have to run and hide, the hidden caches will give me a better chance of making it.

In the case of a natural disaster where help will eventually arrive but you have to leave for your immediate safety (say a hurricane is heading your way) would a friend or family member in a distant town take you in? A "disaster buddy" in another area is a good idea. You need someone who is reachable in a few hours' drive, someone with whom you have already made plans such that if a disaster happens in your area, you can go to his place to wait it out and vice versa.

A government shelter is not for me thank you. I want to stay out of the FEMA camps. Who wants to be dependent on the government for their survival anyways? I am one of those "wrong-headed" Americans who would rather trust his own wits and skills than the government to take care of me after a disaster. They just hate that.

Bug out Bag Contents

Okay, so what should be included in a bug out bag? Well, that depends on you. You will have to consider things like your location, where you are going, your health, your skills, and time of the year. There is no one bug out bag list that fits all needs and individuals.

However, by looking at the bug out bag lists put together by a number of different people, you can get some good ideas to suit your bug out bag for your personal location and needs.

What is In My Bug out Bag

Okay, since we are talking about bug out bag lists, I am sure that you are probably wondering what is in my bug out bag. Well, I will show you. Below are photos of my bug out bag contents. I hope that the photos will help you put together your own bug out bag.

Tools: including Glock Shovel, Mora "Light My Fire" knife, Bowie Knife and multi-tool.

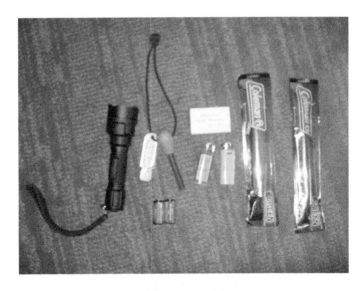

Light and Fire Making Items

First Aid-Kit

Battery, Solar and Crank Power Radio. Dollar Bill Shown for Size Comparison

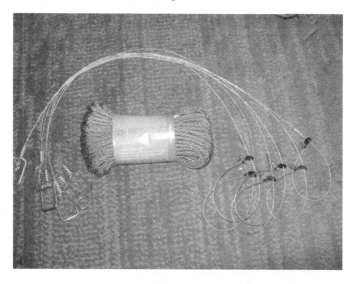

Binding, and Snaring – aka Rope and Snares.

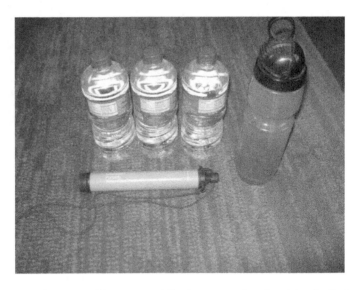

Bottled water, Lifestraw, and Berkey water bottle with a built-in filter.

Food items should be lightweight, provide essential nutrients, and be suitable for long-term storage of one year or more. I replace my bug out bag food every year...

Personal hygiene items: Soap, Toothpaste, Brush, Toilet Paper.

Chow Time. Do not forget to Include Cooking and Eating Utensils
in your Bug out Bag.

A Sewing Kit is Necessary for Your Bug out Bag.

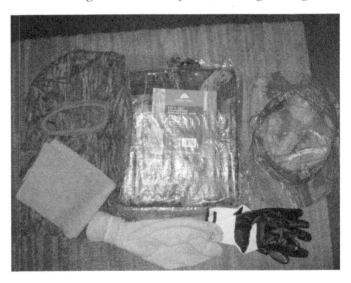

Bonnie Hat, Lightweight Work Gloves, Extra Socks, 8'x10' Tarp
and Head net

Outdoor Survival Kit, Compass, Extra Flashlight, Batteries, and Camo Compact.

Alternate Contents List

This is my list of bug out bag items from my pack in 2012 – you will note that a few items overlap with my current list above. I included this alternative list for a couple of reasons: (1) to give you more ideas on what to include in your BOB, and (2) to show you how packs of this type "evolve" over time. You will be constantly removing and adding different items over time.

- The Pack - I have an LC-1 "Alice" pack but any quality pack with enough capacity will do. Stick with camouflage, dark green or other natural colors that blend with the terrain.
- Water - A canteen with cup and cover for your belt, water bottle, and a good portable filter.
- Fire - Waterproof matches, a magnesium fire starter, and tender.

- Food - Pack enough to last five to seven days. Rice, oatmeal, beef jerky, energy bars, etc. Another option is MREs and the freeze-dried foods often sold to campers and hikers. Choose foods that are lightweight and have a suitable shelf life.

- Stove - A small stove is essential if you want to stay hidden. Smoke and noise from the cutting and burning of wood would be undesirable if you were in hostile territory or pursued by an aggressor. I have a Peak- 1 backpackers stove. There are others but this is what I have and can recommend.

- Sleeping bag - If you are in a cold area a good sleeping bag could mean the difference between life and death. Get a lightweight "mummy" style bag rated to -20 degrees.

- Shelter - Rain poncho, tarp, or compact tent. Stick with natural colors that blend with the surrounding area.

- Cooking - I have a Stainless Steel 5-Piece Mess Kit that I ordered from amazon.com. However, any lightweight kit will do.

- First Aid Kit - It is best to assemble your own kit, tailored to your individual needs. If you are lazy you can purchase a ready-made kit. Do not forget to add personal meds.

- Light - I have a 2-AA Cell Mini LED Flashlight and a 9-Hour Candle.

- Tools - A folding saw, Swiss Army pocketknife and fixed blade knife. A lightweight shovel and machete are nice but add extra weight.

- Extra Clothing - At least one extra pair of socks and underwear. Add other items if you feel the need and have space.

- Fishing Kit - Line, hooks and sinkers, and a few small lures. I also have a small gill net for catching fish.

- <u>Snare Wire</u> - I make my own from copper wire. Do not forget to include at least 50 ft. of parachute cord.
- <u>Plastic Bags</u> - Two or three large lawn bags and several zip-lock sandwich bags can be used for a number of tasks and to keep things dry.
- <u>Small Binoculars</u> - See wild game and enemy before they can see you.
- <u>Sewing Kit</u> - Needle and thread do not forget to include a few extra buttons.
- <u>This 'n' That</u> - Head net, electrical tape, face paint, gloves, sharpening stone, etc.

Lifestraw Water Filter Perfect Addition for the Bug Out Bag

In my bug out bag, I have two Sport Berkey water bottles; these work great and besides filtering out waterborne pathogenic bacteria and heavy metals, the bottles do double duty as a canteen of sorts. However, with clean water being second in importance only to oxygen for survival, I have added yet another water filtration system to my bug out bag.

For utility, I have divided my bug out bag into two separate bags, a full-sized backpack being the main bag and a smaller pack (a US PeaceKeeper Rapid Deployment Pack) for essential items; you know the stuff that you cannot live without.

With the two bag system, it is easy to hide the larger bag or leave it at camp while still allowing me to have those "must have survival items" on my person at all times without having to carry the weight and bulk of the full-sized bag.

While the Berkey bottles are great for a full-sized bug out bag they take up too much space in the smaller bag, so I've added the LifeStraw water filter system to my bug out kit.

The LifeStraw removes 99.9999% of waterborne bacteria, 99.9% waterborne protozoan parasites, and will filter approximately 264 gallons of water.

When I received the LifeStraw in the mail, the first thing I noticed when I opened the package was its weight or lack of it. At 9 inches long with a 1-inch width, it weighs about as much as a pack of cigarettes, but instead of killing, you with toxins the LifeStraw could save your life by eliminating them.

When using the LifeStraw for the first time, it takes a bit of work to get the water flowing up through the filter but once you get the water moving through the straw it is easy to keep it going and to continue drinking.

My only complaints are that I would have liked to have color options when purchasing (a nice olive drab would have been nice). Overall, I think the LifeStraw will be a great addition to any bug out bag.

Thoughts on Specific Bug out Bag Firearms

Most people will suggest a .22 caliber rifle, such as the Ruger 10/22 and this is a great choice. A .22 caliber rifle can take small game as well as larger game such as deer with proper shot placement.

Another advantage for having a .22 Long rifle is the relatively low report especially when using CB caps and the ability to be effectively silenced with a homemade sound suppressor aka "silencer". Just remembered that such a device is illegal without proper government approval and will land you in jail if caught. It is suggested here for a worst-case scenario and only or after you have gone through all of the legal hoops.

The downside of the .22 long rifle round is a limited range, penetration and stopping power, all of which limit the round's effectiveness when used for self-defense. I suggest a backup handgun chambered for a cartridge suitable for self-defense. I would not go below a 9 mm or 38 special. I would then use good expanding ammo.

Even with a 9mm and 38 special you should seriously consider using only the +P rounds such as the 115 or 124 grain JHP +P in the 9 mm or 158-grain lead semi-wadcutter hollow point .38 Special +P for defensive purposes.

Your location would also determine your choice of weapons. For example, those bugging-out in grizzly country should definitely consider something more powerful than the aforementioned 9 mm or 38 special.

My first choice for protection against such large game would be a center-fire rifle chambered for 308 or larger. My second choice would be a magnum revolver with a 5.5" to 7.5" barrel chambered for .44 magnums or larger.

It is wise to avoid any armed confrontation if possible. Trust me you are not a coward if you avoid the possibility of being shot or having to shoot someone else. You are not expendable and neither are the lives of your family or those in your bug out-group. Those with the macho kill 'em all attitude will not last very long after the balloon goes up.

With that said, a semi-auto military style rifle should be considered especially if you are trying to get from an urban area to the country where facing organized gangs or other threats attempting to block your exit could be a possibility.

An AR-15 with collapsible buttstock or folding stocked AK-47 (for compactness and concealability) could help get you out of a dangerous situation if pressed into one while taking up little space and not adding significant weight to your overall survival gear.

Chapter 7

TOOLS FOR SELF-DEFENSE AND FORAGING

In this chapter, we will be talking about tools for self-defense, hunting, trapping and other tools and gear needed for foraging for food. I will try to keep this as short and to the point as possible while still covering everything that you really need to know in order to make an informed decision when buying and learning how to use these tools to feed yourself and your family.

Shotguns

No foraging arsenal would be complete without at least one shotgun. By simply changing shot loads or moving up to slugs the shotgun can be used to take every game and predatory animal in North America out to 100 yards. In addition, let us not forget that a pump-action or semi-automatic shotgun loaded with buckshot or slugs makes an excellent self-defense tool, especially if the shooter knows how to use it to its maximum effectiveness.

The shotgun that you choose for foraging purposes need not be expensive; the simple single-shot break-action shotgun is an excellent tool for the forager. They can be purchased new for under $200 in most areas, and are lightweight and extremely rugged and reliable.

Add a carry sling and a way to carry some extra ammo. I like the Voodoo Tactical Shotgun Shell Ammo Pouch. With this, you are ready to go foraging for small game, foul or even larger game if the opportunity should present itself.

Ammo selection will, of course, depend on what you are hunting; I like to keep several different types in my sling loops, where I can quickly get to it and change out one round for another if needed.

Say, for example, that I am hunting rabbit and happen to spot a deer in the distance. It is a simple matter to quietly and quickly switch from a chambered shot-shell (I like #6 shot for small game) to a rifled slug and effectively and humanely take the deer.

For self-defense purposes I suggest a pump-action or semi-automatic (I prefer the pump-action but there are also some good semi-autos available) shotgun in 12 gauge; however, for smaller shooters a 20 gauge will suffice. There are so many great brands and models available that it would take several chapters to go into any detail on each. Therefore, I will not waste your time doing that here.

Two of my favorite pump-action shotgun manufacturers are Remington and Mossberg. My personal home defense shotgun is a Mossberg model 590 with ghost ring sights and speed fed stock. In my opinion, as a certified gunsmith the Mossberg 590 is the best "out of the box" pump-action defensive shotgun available today.

.22 Rifles

No survival "arsenal" would be complete without at least one high-quality .22lr caliber rifle. Because there are literally hundreds of quality brands and models available, I will not take up your time by trying to go over the details of each one here. I will instead mention several of my personal favorites.

My first choice for a semi-auto .22lr would be the Ruger 10/22 takedown model; this is essentially the same rifle as the super trusted and reliable standard 10/22 but with the ability to be taken apart for transport and storage.

My first choice for a bolt-action .22lr is the Ruger American Rimfire Standard Bolt-Action with 18-inch barrel. It is well made with fewer parts to break than a semi-automatic and I have found it to be more accurate out-of-the-box than any standard out-of-the-box semiauto .22lr that I have tested it against.

Another one of my favorite .22lr rifles is the Smith and Wesson MP 15/22. Mine has been ultra-reliable after thousands of rounds and is a perfect training tool for new shooters or for cheap live-fire practice for AR-15 owners. However, it is not my first choice when small game hunting. The .22lr that most often accompanies me on small game hunts is the Ruger American .22lr mentioned above.

My first choice when adding an optical sight (scope) to a .22lr is the Nikon ProStaff Rimfire 4 x 32 Black Matte Riflescope. I have tried other cheaper (and a few more expensive) alternatives when scoping .22lr rifles and found the Nikon ProStaff to be the best option.

Centerfire Rifles

Here again, I will not waste your time by trying to cover 101 different manufacturers and models of centerfire rifles. Again, I will instead elaborate on my two of my personal favorites.

For hunting larger game in my state of Tennessee, I do not need anything more powerful than a .308 win. However if you live in grizzly and moose country you may want to move up to something like a .338 magnum to ensure a clean and humane kill.

My first choice for a .308 semi-auto is the Smith and Wesson M&P 10. The M&P 10 is built on an AR type platform with a standard 20 round magazine. I have found it to be a well-made, accurate, and reliable rifle. It can be used for both hunting large game and as a main battle rifle. However, the current, 2015 price tag of over $1,600 will no doubt be a roadblock for many. (I had to save for almost a year to afford it.)

My first choice for a bolt-action .308 is the Ruger Gunsite Scout Rifle but with a standard rear mounted optic sight instead of the forward mounted "scout" configuration.

All of my .308's are topped with the Nikon ProStaff 3-9 x 40 Black Matte Riflescope (BDC) optics and have backup standard iron sights and a sling. If you are serious about using a rifle for the defense of your property and for hunting, please get a copy of The Art of the Rifle by the late Jeff Cooper. A great book that is full of tips and advice will help to increase on target proficiency.

Handguns

This is one of those subjects that I hate to even get into here and one that I purposely avoid discussing in public because it never ends without someone getting their feelings hurt. And that is because nearly everyone has his or her favorites and is unwilling to consider anything else.

So like we've already done above, instead of going into a hundred different manufacturers and models, I'll simply tell you my favorites that have proven effective for me after years of shooting, hunting, plinking, and competition.

We will start with the .22lr, of which my favorite is the Browning Buckmark. This is the top .22lr handgun made today, period. I have carried mine all over the forests of Appalachia, and can shoot it accurately enough to make headshots on cottontail rabbits at 50 yards.

I have no idea how many rounds that I have put through mine but it has to be ten thousand or more and I have never had a failure that was not ammo related.

Another excellent .22lr handgun is the Beretta 21A Bobcat. The Bobcat is not ideal for small game hunting or self-defense. But it's weight and compact size will allow you to have it on you at all times and any handgun that you have with you is better that the one you left at home or back at camp because it was too large, heavy and inconvenient to carry.

I carry mine when I'm on the river fishing, camping, hunting ginseng or just working around the homestead. It's weight and size make it easy to go armed at all times. The Israeli Mossad has proven the effectiveness of the .22lr as an offensive/defensive tool with its use of the Beretta 70 in .22lr. Israeli Sky Marshals also carry the Beretta 70.

Glock makes by far my favorite centerfire handguns. However, they are not the only quality choice on the market. There are many different handgun manufacturers that have products worth considering. The most important consideration is to purchase the handgun that fits your hand best. If the handgun fits your hand correctly, you will naturally shoot it more accurately.

Out of the Glock line up my favorite model is the Glock model 19. The Glock 19 is a medium-sized 9mm handgun that is the perfect size for open carry in a belt holster, yet small enough to be carried comfortably concealed under summer clothes. Another plus is that the Glock 19 has a 15 round magazine capacity, which is comparable with other, larger and heavier 9mm handguns such as the Berretta 92.

When it comes to ammo choices and "stopping power" there are just as many opinions as there are for handgun choices. However, my personal carry load in a 9mm round is the Corbon 115-grain +p. Ballistics for this round is close to those produced by the 357 magnums and it is a proven stopper according to both ballistic research and actual real-life use.

Air Rifles

Air rifles are often overlooked by survival planners and this is unfortunate because they have a lot to offer with the most notable being the ability to quietly take small game out to approximately 35 yards.

However, to get this kind of performance from an air rifle, you're going to have to look past the $45 models like those often seen at Walmart. These don't produce the energy or velocity that is needed to cleanly take small game. You will probably have to spend over $150 at current prices before getting one that will do take small game effectively.

A personal favorite and the one that I have taken the largest number of small game with is the Benjamin Titan GP Nitro Piston .22 caliber air rifle. I have found the .22 caliber air rifles to provide much better on target effeteness i.e. dropping a small game animal in their tracks than those in .177.

The Benjamin Titan GP .22 caliber air rifle features a 19 inch fully rifled barrel and a muzzle brake, both with a nice looking deep blued steel finish. I also have a Ruger .177 caliber air rifle and comparatively the finish on both the metal and stock is much nicer on the Titan GP.

As with most air rifles of this type, the Titan GP has no iron sights but the rifle is grooved for mounting an optical sight. The addition of a good set of metal sights would greatly add to the overall functionality and dependability of the rifle.

However, as a rule, I prefer all of my rifles to have the choice of iron sights as well as scope mounting with see through mounts. Scopes can break, become fogged, lose zero, etc., and the ability to quickly change from one sighting option to the other without losing the target aids greatly to the utility of any rifle.

The Titan GP features an ambidextrous thumbhole stock with dual raised cheekpieces, and while well designed, I found the reach from the grip to the trigger to be a bit long. However, this would not be a problem for shooters with larger hands or longer fingers. Even with the longer reach to the trigger from the grip, I have no problem pulling the trigger or shooting the rifle.

The rifle also has a 2-stage adjustable trigger for fine-tuning to the needs of each shooter; however, I found the factory setting to be very good for my needs so I left the settings as is. However, the adjustment is an option and a welcome addition that I am sure many will find very useful.

One of the main selling points of the Benjamin Titan is the Nitro Piston system and a velocity of up to 950 FPS. The Nitro Piston offers several advantages over rifles with a metal mainspring system, such as smoother cocking, no spring fatigue, reduced vibration, functions well in cold weather and the Nitro Piston system is also much quieter.

In fact, the Titan is noticeably quieter than my other air rifles and is much quieter than my Ruger air rifle, which is the loudest of the lot.

Bows, Arrows, and Blow Guns

I have used blowguns for hunting small game since I was in my early teens and I can assure you that there are not toys, far from it. In practiced hands (and lungs), the blowgun can be used very effectively, to take small game and are much more accurate and deadly than the slingshot.

There are currently three sizes of marketed blowguns in the U.S. one in .40 caliber, .50 caliber, and .625 caliber diameters. Each has different advantages over the other. I personally prefer the .40 caliber versions because I have found that I can shoot them further with more accurately and have not noted any difference in effectiveness when taking small game.

Fortunately, blowguns are priced so cheaply that you can buy several (or make your own) to see what works best for you. If you're interested in finding out a wealth of information on blowguns and how to make your own Michael Janich has an excellent book available to help you. It is called Blowguns: The Breath of Death by Michael Janich and covers everything blowgun related.

Another favorite weapon for foraging is the bow and arrow. In skilled hands, the bow and arrow can be used to take both large and small game, and like with the blowgun you can make your own. However, it is likely that nothing that you can make in the home workshop will compare to the power and velocity of commercially manufactured compound and crossbows.

Bows are like handguns in that you should try out several before deciding what works best for you. Personally, I prefer a more traditional recurve bow with a 45-pound draw weight to a compound but that is a personal choice and only one that you can make after gaining experience.

Chapter 8

URBAN SURVIVAL CONSIDERATIONS

The Get Back Home Urban Survival Kit

Most of you probably have a bug out bag by now. If not then go back and re-read the chapter on bug out bags and put one together. Having a bug out bag is good insurance in the event you are forced to evacuate your home or retreat for some unforeseen reason.

It seems most preppers have planned to bug out but few of have even considered the need to find their way back home if caught away during an emergency. You not only need a bug out bag, you also need a get back home back.

No doubt, many of you spend a lot of time away from home--with work, school, and business sometimes taking you hundreds of miles away from home. Most of the time this is not an issue for me but recently I have had to make several trips with my girlfriend to take her father to the cancer specialist on the other side of the state.

What would we do if disaster struck while we were several hundred miles from home? What would we do in the event of a terrorist attack, riot, earthquake, or similar disaster? Could we get back home? What would we do if forced to stay in the area for several days or even weeks?

With any luck, I will be able to drive out but you never know; the roads could be blocked or impassable because of damage, the area could be quarantined or it could be too dangerous to move for several days.

As with anything related to survival, there are no guarantees and I doubt her father could make it under anything but the best of conditions considering his health. I just hope nothing bad happens with him in tow.

To increase our odds of making it back or surviving in the city, if needed, I have put together a "Get Home Kit" that I take on extended trips. Sure, I could have just taken my bug out bag, but it really is not the best solution and the gear for the most part. It is not what I would need in an urban setting.

The basic needs of water, shelter, food and medical are the same in the wilderness or city but the means of attainment are different in most cases. My bug out bag was put together for an extended trip to the woods where I can make most of what I need from what Mother Nature has to offer.

If trapped in the city, I may have to scrounge or steal most of what we need to survive, especially if we are forced to stay and survive for an extended period. No, I am not advocating theft or looting but I am not above it if the other alternative is starvation or death.

My get home kit is smaller than my bug out bag and weighs considerably less. Everything fits snugly inside a small dark gray and green backpack that I bought at the local flea market for five dollars. I intentionally averted from camo or military type packs to avoid attracting attention.

Now that we know why we need a get home pack, the question remains what do we pack in our urban survival kit.

Get Home Urban Survival Kit Contents

- A fixed blade knife (Glock Knife)
- Multi-tool (Gerber Recoil Auto-Plier)
- Two Small Bic Lighters

- One Box Water Proofed Wooden Matches
- Two Berkey Water Bottles
- Small LED flashlight (Maglite XL100)
- Cell Phone
- Prepaid Calling Card
- Lock Pick (Dyno Kwik Pick)
- First Aid Tactical Trauma Kit
- Antibacterial Hand Wipes
- Space Blanket
- Bag Of Trail Mix, Box of Power Bars (15) And Electrolyte Packets
- Detailed Map Of Area And Compass
- Garmin Handheld GPS Navigator
- OC Spray
- One Hundred Dollars In small Bills (1's -5's and 10's)
- Glock 19 and 200 + rounds of Ammunition, and 2 or More Ammo Magazines.

Aside from and in addition to the get home kit, I pack a large cooler with food and drinks for the trip, partly for emergencies but mainly because I am cheap and do not want to waste money buying fast food along the way. I also carry sleeping bags in my vehicle during winter along with my winter emergency car kit and a full toolbox.

Surviving Long-Term In the City After a Collapse

Even if you are fortunate enough to have a retreat in the country, getting to your safe haven may be impossible during the upheaval. Roads blocked by wrecked and fuel-less vehicles will stop most people who are bugging out in their tracks. Maybe you were born lucky and can make it out safely before the balloon bursts. But then what?

People in rural areas will start shooting if threatened by mobs of refugees fleeing the city. Do not expect to be welcomed with arms outstretched? Most country folks do not trust outsiders. You will most likely be greeted with a load of buckshot, not the cup of fresh coffee and meaningful conversation you had hoped for.

After the cities are in ruins, criminal gangs will start to migrate into surrounding rural areas (especially known farming areas) where they will continue their business of stealing, raping and terrorizing in more fruitful territory (when selecting a rural retreat location get as far away from urban areas and main roads as possible).

If you cannot or will not get out of your urban location <u>now</u>, at least, start making plans to survive the best that you can where you are. It will not be easy but it can be done.

Food

You should store enough food to last at least six months. More than one year would be ideal but probably impossible for most exurbanites because of limited storage space. This means enough food to live on without leaving home. As discussed in Chapter 2, food staples include rice, beans, honey, wheat, sugar, tea, coffee, salt, pepper, baking soda, cooking oil, etc. In addition, canned soups, meats, fruits, and vegetables should be included for variety. A food storage calculator is an excellent tool for approximating needed qualities of foods and is a great help here.

Also, see my recent article at TheSurvivalistBlog.net – How to Get a Family of Four Prepped for The Coming Collapse – In the Quickest and Easiest Way Possible - for a full list of supplies and gear.

Sprouting seeds for fresh greens is a very important urban survival skill that will keep you supplied with fresh greens even in the winter. Sprouts are germinated seeds of vegetables, nuts, grains, and legumes. Sprouts are nutritious, inexpensive, and high in protein. Sprouts should be included in your survival food plans. All that is needed are a couple of quart mason jars, some nylon window screen, rubber bands, and viable seed stock.

If you decide to include whole grains in your diet, you will need a grain mill. All chosen grain mills should have changeable heads so you can use both steel and stone heads for grinding depending on the product being milled. Some people suggest that steel-burred grinders cause heat that could damage the nutrient content of the grain. Do not buy into that. Hand grinding does not cause enough heat to cause damage.

Next, you will need something to cook with; I recommend one of the Coleman multi-fuel camp stoves. I have a Coleman Exponent Multi-Fuel Stove, which burns both unleaded gasoline and kerosene. These stoves are small, lightweight, and very energy-efficient.

Remember when using stoves like the Coleman camp stoves indoors the fumes must be vented to the outside; if not carbon monoxide can build up and kill you, especially in a small or confined area.

In most cases, an open window near the cooking area will suffice for ventilation. Read and follow the instructions in the provided owner's manual.

My top recommendation for outdoor cooking (cooking outdoors may attract unwanted attention) is the EcoZoom rocket stove. Click on the link to read my full review.

If you do not have one already go by your local shopping center and pick up a Stanley Aladdin narrow-mouth thermos bottle. You will use the thermos as an energy-efficient appliance for cooking. Don't get a wide-mouthed thermos, if you intend to use it for cooking. I have found that these are less efficient at holding heat. (Some of the better wide-mouths thermoses may work well enough, but I still prefer the Stanley Aladdin narrow-mouth thermos bottle.)

It is best to use a different bottle for cooking than your everyday thermos. Coffee smell, for instance, tends to leach into whatever you are cooking even if the bottle has been cleaned.

Thermos cooking is in no way difficult or complicated. All you need is some simple directions.

Water

Without a source of clean drinking water, most of us will die within three to seven days, depending on individual health, weather conditions, and workload. The problem with water is it is difficult to store enough to last through an extended emergency and living in an urban apartment makes it nearly impossible.

Collecting rainwater on the roofs of buildings could be a solution in areas that receive an ample amount rainfall. Use plastic sheeting, tarps, etc., to funnel water into clean trashcans, buckets, kiddie pools or other suitable containers.

When I lived in an apartment building years ago, I bought several "kiddie pools" just for this purpose. They can be stored neatly stacked one inside the other and slid under the bed out of the way until needed.

Some urban areas have lakes or streams nearby but these will be polluted and contaminated. A running water source is better but still no guarantee of cleanliness. Never drink directly from the source. There is no way of knowing if the water is contaminated (it mostly will be) without proper testing. Do not take chances. Invest in a good water filter to be sure. The best filters filter out bacteria, chemicals and rotozoa (Giardia) and viruses.

Shelter

I hated living in an apartment. I felt as if I had no privacy whatsoever. I could hear every word, whimper, moan, or scream through the walls, ceiling, and floor. I am sure everyone in the building felt the same way. If you are stuck in a large city, an apartment is likely the situation you will need to deal with despite its limitations.

There are a few things that you can do to make your place more secure from break-ins and home invasion. The first thing I did was replace the front door with a steel security door with deadbolt and peephole (same color and look of the old door). I hid the old door in the closet and replaced it when I moved. I also replaced the door leading into the bedroom with the same type door, lock, and peephole set up for an instant safe-room (safer) inside the apartment.

Do not forget smoke and carbon monoxide. Keep at least two fully charged fire extinguishers on hand at all times. In addition, the magnetic break door and window alarms work well when used to guard the windows and doors leading into the apartment.

If you are above the first floor, an escape ladder or rope should be kept under the bed or other easy to get to location in case of fire as well as an emergency escape hood.

When you rent, you are always faced with the possibility of eviction if you cannot pay. If possible, keep the rent paid up, at least, six months. If you have no other way of paying in advance, borrowing the money from the bank will keep you sheltered during hard times. I hate debt but this is one area where it could be to your advantage depending on your personal circumstances and how you work the situation.

Going mobile and living in an RV could be an option for the city survivor. But fuel will likely become a problem post collapse. Like everything else in life, we must weigh the good against the bad and make our choices based on that knowledge.

Weapons

Defense in the city will likely be a short-range engagement. For urban areas, I recommend a good pump action 12 gauge shotgun and a handgun. The Mossberg 500/590 or Remington 870 are both excellent choices. For versatility put back a variety of shotshell loadings as well as buckshot and rifled slugs.

Handguns should be at least .38 caliber or above. I like both revolvers and automatics. In skilled hands, both can be effective. Stay with what you know and practice. If you have had little or no training in this area seek out a competent instructor and become qualified. If you are fortunate enough to live in a state that issues concealed carry permits you should apply for yours as soon as possible.

My favorite foraging tool in urban areas is an air gun or blow gun. The blowgun has the advantage of not looking like a weapon so is less likely to attract unwanted attention.

Wild Game

In urban areas, you will have small game such as rabbit and squirrel but what most people fail to realize is that the outskirts of most urban areas harbor a good number of whitetail deer. The trouble is that everyone will be hunting so the numbers of wild game may be depleted quickly and let us not overlook the danger of going out to hunt in those areas.

Small game can be taken with traps, air rifles, slingshots or even with a club or rock under the right circumstances. When I lived on a lot in a small city, I shot squirrels that found their way into my back lot with a .22 caliber rifle loaded with CB caps (down-loaded .22 Rimfire ammo). The little rounds are very quiet and can take most small animals out to about ten yards.

Most cities have an abundant pigeon population. It is a simple matter to follow the flock to their roost at dusk. Shining a light into their eyes, they tend to sit still where they can be caught or killed with little trouble. Air guns and slingshots work well.

Without a doubt, the most abundant source of meat in any urban environment is the common rat. They have thrived under even the most challenging circumstances. It is almost a certainty if there are human survivors after any catastrophe rats will be in abundance but likely infested with parasites and other things that could make you sick and, therefore, should be used only as a last resort to avoid death from starvation. Like most small animals, they can be trapped in homemade box traps or shot.

Urban Gardening

Do not expect to support yourself entirely from a city garden at least not at first. I have raised tomatoes in a window box and hanging baskets on the terrace. Perhaps given enough time, large community gardens would be put in place and these could be worked by groups of urban survivors.

During the first months preceding a total collapse gardens will need to be hidden and out of site. Many vegetables (especially among most city dwellers who think vegetables come from the supermarket) are easily mistaken for weeds and are not very difficult to keep hidden from passers-by.

The first rule of avoiding detection is to never plant your crops using the traditional row method. The three sisters gardening method comes to mind. Some Native American tribes used this technique to grow corn, beans and squash to great effect and it acts as a natural camouflage.

When it comes to survival gardening obviously we must start with a seed. Therefore, it becomes a necessity to have a source of viable seed on hand. Look for non-hybrid ("heirloom") varieties. You want to be sure the seed saved from year to year will produce true and continue to do so. Hybrid varieties, for the most part, are unpredictable and generally only do well during the first year of planting.

Include such vegetables as artichoke, asparagus, beans, beets, broccoli, cabbage, carrots, cauliflower, celery, chives, corn, cucumber, eggplant, garlic, gourds, kale, leeks, lettuce, mustard green, onions, parsley, parsnips, peanuts, peas, peppers, pumpkin, radishes, soybeans, spinach, squash, sunflowers, Swiss chard, tomatoes, turnip, watermelon, zucchini, etc. In general put back seeds that grow well in your area and for foods, you like to eat.

Even in the most populated areas after the rioting, burning and looting stops, there will be survivors. The most difficult part is surviving the first few months after the crash. After that, the rebuilding can begin.

Chapter 9

MEDICAL CONSIDERATIONS

Disclaimer: I am not a doctor and cannot give medical advice, diagnosis or suggest treatment for any sickness or disease. All information in this chapter is for informational purposes only. Please seek out a competent medical care professional for any injury, sickness, or disease that you might have.

Now that the legal disclaimer is out of the way, let us get started with some general info and advice on the types of injuries you can expect, and with a discussion of medical kits and contents, references and training recommendations.

Most preppers when stockpiling medical kits and medications often make the mistake of targeting the bulk of their preparations toward trauma care--i.e. treating gunshot wounds and other trauma caused by violence or accident.

While having the medical skills and tools to treat such injuries is a must there needs to be a balance between those types supplies and supplies needed for more likely medical conditions such as the common cold, flu, dehydration, diarrhea, food poisoning, arthritis, heat stroke, hypothermia, diabetes, childbirth and so forth.

Most of the above types of illnesses are easy to deal with while the medical system is running smoothly. However, after just a short-term disaster the medical system is often overburdened and is hard pressed to meet the increased demand causing treatment to become degraded or nonexistent.

If the medical system cannot efficiently deal with the demand for treatment after a short-term disaster, one can only imagine the lack of care that we will experience following a major event such as an EMP, a nuclear attack or a cyber attack that shuts down the power grid for months or even a viral pandemic that affects millions nationwide.

After an economic collapse, the main hurdle to getting medical care might be the inability to pay the upfront admittance costs rather than a lack of available care.

I also expect the quality of care to decline in the months after an economic collapse. In other words, you might be able to find an office or hospital that will accept you (if you have the admittance fee), but the care you get maybe far below current standards.

After Argentina's economic collapse it was common for hospitals to ask patients to bring their own medical supplies when they needed care. As a side note, medical supplies make great barter items. It is also a good idea to have a supply of silver coins to pay for admittance into a doctor's office or emergency room.

Prevention

Prevention involves regular exercise and proper diet. This is one of those things that some preppers seem to ignore. Or perhaps they're just too lazy and undisciplined to get into better shape. You know the ones--they buy all of the best gear and cool gadgets, and they pack their bug out bags, thinking they are ready for the "big one". Sadly, most of these folks cannot carry their gear 100 yards without stopping for a snack and thirty-minute nap.

Getting into decent shape (no you do not have to be a top contender in the next iron man triathlon) is one of the best things that you can do for yourself now and it will benefit you greatly in any disaster.

At a minimum strive to meet the fitness and agility level presented in the chart below--after consulting with your doctor first of course. We do not want anyone with any preexisting medical conditions to fall over with a heart attack, so please go get a check-up and ask your doctor if you are healthy enough for this type of physical activity.

FITNESS REQUIREMENT	EVENT
Walk / Run one Mile minutes – 20 minutes if 50+ years of age	In 15
Push-Ups – 25 if you're 50+ years of age	35 reps
Sit-Ups – 30 if you're 50+ years of age	40 reps
Bench Press 75% of body weight – 50% for those 50+	1+ reps

The key to success here is to start slowly, gradually working up to and even beyond the fitness level presented in the chart above. However, those requirements listed will give you a starting point and some goals to strive toward achieving.

For those of you who are already in good physical condition and have no problem performing the exercises listed above, you should continue to stay on a maintenance program to maintain or even surpass what is listed in the chart above.

Okay, now let us look at the steps that necessary (for most people) to get in and stay in reasonable physical condition. Again, nothing here is to be taken or intended as medical advice. Go talk to your doctor and ask him or her about each step in this chapter and if it is right for you and in current physical condition.

Start with a Healthy Diet

A healthy diet should be at the very top of everyone's to-do list, especially if you want to get into better physical condition and be better prepared to survive a disaster. However, where do you start? There is so much information on healthy eating continually filling the pages of books, magazine, and digital media that it is easy to become overwhelmed to the point of just giving up.

When it comes to a healthy diet the most important consideration is to keep it as simple as possible, which is what I intend to do here. Forget about counting calories or portion size. You want to eat better not waste away in hunger. There are three key rules to eating healthy and those are (1) avoid refined sugar, (2) avoid prepackaged foods and (3) avoid fast food.

The healthiest foods that you can eat are those that have been grown and harvested from your own garden. Commercially produced fruits and vegetables cannot compete with the goodness and health boosting benefits that are provided from freshly harvested (preferably organically grown) vegetables and fruits that you have grown yourself in your home garden or orchard. A close second is to purchase produce at your local farmer's market.

The bulk of your diet should consist of fresh fruits and vegetables, chicken, eggs, fish, grass fed beef, venison other wild game, grains, beans and olive oil. Also, remember to chew your food slowly and completely. By chewing your food slowly you will get full on less food and help your digestion. Eat until you feel full and then stop.

Vitamin and Mineral Supplements

Listed below are two books that I recommend you add to your bookshelf for further study:

- Prescription for Nutritional Healing, Fifth Edition: A Practical A-to-Z Reference to Drug-Free Remedies Using Vitamins, Minerals, Herbs & Food Supplements by Phyllis A. Balch CNC
- Over the Counter Natural Cures: Take Charge of Your Health in 30 Days with 10 Lifesaving Supplements for under $10 by Shane Ellison.

These two books will cover everything that you need to know about vitamins, natural healing, and health.

So what vitamins and supplements do I take? Every day I swallow a Centrum Silver® Adults 50+ multivitamin and mineral, 500 mg of vitamin C, Curcumin C3 Complex 500 mg, and 1200 mg of fish oil capsules. This is the combination that I have found that works best for me as a guy. However, each person has individual needs. I do recommend that women talk to their doctors about calcium and vitamin D. What is good for me might not be for you. As with diet, it is best to keep it simple. If you are taking more five different supplements per day then you are probably taking too many (unless, of course, you are talking them on the recommendation of your physician).

Get enough Sleep

According to the National Sleep Foundation, an average adult needs 7-9 hours of sleep per calendar day for optimum health and alertness. Granted this much sleep will probably be non-existent after a disaster. However, note that this chapter is about getting into better shape now before a disaster strikes. Getting in shape now will help you be more prepared and able to handle whatever might come your way.

The key to getting good night's sleep is to set a regular schedule to go to bed and get up and stick to it. A regular schedule will help your body knows when it is time to go to sleep and when it is time to get up. Set a sleep schedule and stick to it.

Another key ingredient that I have found that works wonders when trying to get a good nights sleep valerian root, specifically Spring Valley Natural Valerian Root sold by Wal-Mart.

Valerian root has several sedative compounds to help you relax and fall asleep faster, and it has been proven non-toxic with zero addictive properties.

It is also important to relax and take it easy. Relaxation will improve your sleep patterns as well as your overall health. It has been documented by countless studies and in a number of medical journals that stress has a detrimental effect on our overall health. Stressed for long periods can affect blood pressure, blood sugar levels, the immune system, and can cause premature aging, heart disease, and even cancer.

I know it can be difficult to relax after you have opened your eyes to the true state of the world and understand what is at stake. The pressure to do something and to do more to prepare can be overwhelming at times but it is important to take a step back every now and then to relax.

I take two days per week that I do not (or try not to) think about the sad shape of the world, politics or prepping. I take those two days to just relax and spend time with family, go fishing, sit in the swing, watch a movie or go for a long drive and pray. I just take the time to relax no matter what is going on in the world around me.

Let us get physical

First, before you start any type of physical activity, you should schedule an appointment with your doctor for a complete health check-up, and get permission to proceed from there before you start working out or even getting out of bed.

So what types of exercises should you be doing that will help you to better defend your retreat? Well, to be honest that depends on your current level of physical conditioning and how physically fit that you want to be. No one can be too physically fit and most of us will have to continually work at it to see improvement and to even retain the gains that we make.

Any fitness program should start with flexibility. Stretch before and after every workout. Stretch your legs, back, arms, shoulders and neck. The most important thing to remember is to take it slow. Do not over-stretch. Always stretch with solid, non-bouncy movements. This will help you avoid injury and setbacks.

Strength Training

While you could join a gym and train three or more times per week, most preppers will find that working out at home can have just as much benefit as joining a gym plus working out at home will save money on membership fees and the expense of travel to and from the work-out facility. This money can be used to buy other survival preps or even to take the family out for a night on the town.

In fact, you do not even need free weights or any other exercise equipment to build strength and muscle endurance. Calisthenics (bodyweight exercises) if performed correctly and regularly will help you get stronger by building muscle mass.

So what types of calisthenic exercises and routines should you do? The answer to this question will depend on your current physical condition and what you want to achieve. Again as with building flexibility, start slowly to avoid injury and build upon your continued progress each day.

Listed below is a short list of callisthenic exercises to consider when building your routine...

- Push-ups
- Set-ups
- Jumping Jacks
- Squats

- Pull-ups
- Lunges
- Heel raises
- Reverse Push-Ups

I have found it best to not set a number or limit to an individual exercise or movement and instead do each to exhaustion. For example, I'll do one set of push-ups until my muscles are exhausted and can no longer perform the exercise properly, rest for two minutes and repeat two more times. Below is my current calisthenics workout. I call it "the prepper's muscle blast" because, well, it is a blast.

- Push-ups = three sets to exhaustion
- Pull-ups = three sets to exhaustion
- Set-ups = three sets to exhaustion
- Squats = three sets to exhaustion
- Jumping Jacks = 50 reputations

Cardiovascular Endurance Training

Obviously cardiovascular endurance training is the act of exercising to increase endurance. Greater cardiovascular endurance will allow you to work longer and harder. It will allow you to walk and run farther and faster. Building your cardiovascular endurance one of the most important things that you can do to be better prepared to survive a disaster and defend your retreat.

Some folks prefer to run while others prefer to walk at a brisk pace when working to build their cardiovascular endurance. Both will work. However, I prefer to combine both into my cardiovascular endurance training. I also enjoy bicycling. Three days per week, I will walk approximately 200 yards followed by a 100-yard sprint, then walk again for approximately 200 yards followed by a 100-yard sprint and repeat until I have a distance of 1-3 miles, depending on how I feel and how much time I have that day.

In addition, to mix it up a little and prevent boredom, one day per week, I will ride my mountain bike for 4-5 miles non-stop. Usually, I'll ride out to the nearest little country store (a little over 4 miles away) and pick up a couple of things on my shopping list and then ride back home. By riding out to that marketplace, I get exercise for that day, save gas and get some minor shopping done.

The key to building cardiovascular endurance is to make a plan then get off the couch and put that plan into movement. In addition, you have to stick with it… Well, what are you waiting for… hop to it!

Get Medical Training

I have said it before but I will say it again - get as much medical training as possible. Everyone in your family or prepper group should at a minimum, complete a basic CPR and first aid class, and completing paramedic training and or wilderness first aid course would be a great leap forward in your medical preparedness.

If possible, recruit a medical doctor or registered nurse into your group. I know it probably will not be possible for many groups but it will be well worth the effort if you are successful. I know a single guy, who is also a prepper and his number one criteria in choosing a wife is that she be a registered nurse or have other medical training like previous or current work as a paramedic.

Sex Happens

During hard times like those following, an economic collapse or any grid-down situation men and women are going to seek comfort together, and we all know where that leads. That is right, folks. I am talking about intercourse and lots of it.

Keeping that part of human nature in mind you will see the need for lots and lots of birth control. If you are a man who has no plans for children, then getting a vasectomy is a great idea-- problem solved.

Condoms work okay but are not full proof. Consider also that condoms lose their effectiveness as they age. I recommend keeping a year's supply. The number of condoms that you keep in your "years supply" would of course depend on how much sex you plan on having.

Both of the birth control methods mentioned above rely on the male taking the initiative and in my opinion, the vasectomy is by far the best option available for the male. It is permanent and you do not have to keep worrying about having condoms or other types of birth control.

However, a vasectomy does nothing to prevent STDs. If you are married or in a long-term committed relationship and both of you are STD free, then you are good to go.

Women have a much wider selection of birth control methods available to them and I'm not going to get into those here because that would take a full chapter and I'm sure that the ladies reading this already know plenty about the different types of birth control that are available and what works best for them.

The main questions women should ask when looking at post-SHTF birth control methods is what is sustainable? In other words, can you keep it working for months or even a year or more if you could not go back to the doctor to get your prescription refilled.

One long-term birth control method that woman should consider is the IUD, which can be effective for up to 12 years for the non-hormonal type.

As is always the case with medical issues, the best option is to talk to your doctor. Ask her about what long-term birth control methods are available to you before making a decision.

Basic Prepper Medical Kit Recommendations

Having a well-stocked medical kit could mean the difference between life and death.

As you assemble the list of medical items listed below, keep in mind that it is a basic list of suggestions only. Your kit should be tailored to your individual needs. However, the items listed should give you some ideas and get you started in the right direction when putting together your prepper first aid kit.

- Hand soap
- Anti-diarrhea medications
- Bandages and wound dressings (large)
- Basic surgical kit

- Bed liners or plastic sheeting
- Blood pressure monitor
- CPR shields
- Crutches, adjustable
- Epson salts
- Examination gloves
- Antihistamine oral and injectable
- Injectable epinephrine
- IV electrolytes
- Laxatives
- Needles and silk thread for stitching wounds
- Ophthalmic salve
- Oral and injectable antibiotics/sulfas
- Pain medications
- Quikclot clotting agent (or if you prefer Israeli battle dressings)
- Scalpel set if not in surgical kit
- Rubbing alcohol, peroxide, iodine, betadine, (copious amounts)
- SAM splint
- Scissors
- Sterile IV kit
- Sterile needles and syringes
- Stethoscope
- Thermometer (several)
- Tweezers

Personal Items

When putting together your medical kit do not forget to include personal items such as extra eyeglasses, hearing aids and batteries, dentures and prescription medications.

Over The Counter Medications

Having a stockpile of over the counter medications could literally mean the difference between life and death for the prepper in a long-term grid-down situation where re-supply might not be available or as simple as taking a trip to the pharmacy.

Keep in mind that because many over the counter medications have a limited shelf life you will need to date and rotate just as you do with your food stores to ensure a fresh and viable supply. Remember first in, first out to ensure an always-fresh stockpile of perishable items.

When you decide to start stockpiling over the counter medications the first question the arises are "what do I need"? This is a good question because some of this stuff can get rather confusing but it is not at all complicated.

When shopping for over the counter medications keep in mind that the most common illnesses that we currently face will also be the most common after TSHTF, conditions like diarrhea, vomiting, fever, allergy, and pain. These are the main issues that we should prep for and stockpile medications to treat.

Herbs and Supplements

For some medical issues herbal supplements can work better than prescription pharmaceuticals but for disclaimer purposes, I must tell you to please go check with you doctor or other medical professional before going off any prescription medications or starting any supplement program.

Stopping some types of prescription medications "cold turkey" can be deadly. Be smart; talk to your doctor and do your own research before making major decisions pertaining to your health.

What types of herbal medications should you stockpile? Well that depends on your health issues but a few common ones include:

- Hawthorn to lower high blood pressure.
- Garlic, red yeast rice, folic acid, and soluble fiber to lower cholesterol.
- Cinnamon to control blood sugar levels.
- Peppermint oil and ginger for stomach issues like IBS.
- Milk thistle for acute hepatitis, liver disease, jaundice, and gallstones.
- Valerian root extract and melatonin for a restful sleep.
- St. John's wort for depression.

The list could easily grow into another book but it should be enough to get you started. Do your own research and talk to your healthcare provider. An excellent book that is loaded with pertinent information is The Herbal Drugstore by Linda B. White.

Dental Health

Dental health is just as important to your general overall health as is exercise and eating right. It should not be overlooked or downplayed. Take care of your teeth and get regular dental checkups.

I will admit that I am afraid of the dentist. The thought of him grinding, filling and pulling teeth is scary. And let us not forget those horrible shots, bleeding gums and that sucking thing. However, dental emergencies seldom solve themselves. Without medical attention dental issues usually to get worse over time, possibly resulting in dire consequences to your health. Therefore, it is best to get any issues taken care of now.

One thing is certain and that is that dental services will always be in demand. However, like other medical services, they may not be available. Even if dental services are available, you need to ask yourself whether will be able to afford competent care.

This is another instance where I think having a small gold or silver reserve is a good idea. After an economic collapse, the dollar may be worthless or significantly devalued. But gold and silver will retain value and that value that can be traded for dental and medical services in an emergency.

Unfortunately, no matter how prepared we are some dental and medical emergencies cannot be dealt with without proper and professional care. Nevertheless, there are steps that can be taken to better deal with minor problems or to provide care until a real solution can be found.

As previously mentioned preventive maintenance cannot be stressed enough. Take care of your teeth. If possible, visit a dentist at least once a year to find and take care of any problems.

Brush, floss, and rinse. Stock up on oral hygiene supplies. This can be done cheaply compared to the alternative of paying for treatment of major problems brought on by poor oral hygiene. Toothpaste, brushes, rinse and floss would also make excellent barter items, especially in the months following a long-term disaster.

(**Note**) It is easy to make your own toothpaste. Simply mix equal parts baking soda and sea salt. The result tastes awful (you can add peppermint extract to improve taste) until you get used to it but it does a decent job of cleaning your teeth and gums. Simply moisten a toothbrush and dip it in the mixture and brush as usual.

It is a good idea to have a dental first aid kit to complement your other first aid supplies. A basic kit should consist of:

- Temporary filling material Temparin or Cavit

- Tweezers
- Gauze
- Toothbrush
- Soft dental floss
- Toothpaste
- Orajel or another dental pain reliever
- Advil, or Motrin
- Clove Oil (pain relief)
- Rubber gloves (some people are allergic to latex)
- Dental wax
- Toothpicks
- Cotton
- Dental Mirror
- Hand Sanitizer

…and a copy of Where There Is No Dentist by Murray Dickson.

This is a "must have" book. If you do not have a hard copy of this one then your survival library is not complete. Get it now.

Alternatively, if you prefer you can purchase a ready-made kit survival emergency dental care kit and then expand it into a more comprehensive dental care package.

How bad was your last toothache? Now imagine that you have the same pain but no dental care is available.

Shelf Life of Medications

What is the shelf life of medications? This is a tricky subject because there are so many variables to consider such as the type of medication, how old it is when you get it and previous storage conditions. When everything is considered, it becomes impossible to give a specific date as to when a medication will "go bad".

However, most will remain viable well past the listed expiration date.

According to Joseph Alton MD in an article published at TheSurvivalistBlog.net

> FEMA has seen massive stores of medication expire, and so a study was commissioned to find out how effective these expired medications still were. This study is known as the Shelf Life Extension Program (SLEP). This program has evaluated at least 100 medications that were expired for at least 2 to 10 years at the time they were evaluated. This includes many commonly used antibiotics and other medications that could mean the difference between life and death in a collapse situation.

My recommendation is to do your own research and to talk to your doctor about your prescriptions and the shelf life and extended long-term potency of those medications to determine the estimated real-world shelf life of each.

The Use of "Fish Antibiotics" in Humans Post Collapse

The use of fish antibiotics in humans post collapse is another issue that comes up anytime two preppers talk to each other, and for good reason. Without antibiotics, a minor cut or infection can turn deadly.

However, it is often difficult to get a medical doctor to write out a prescription for larger than normal amounts of antibiotics. Fortunately putting back a large stockpile of fish antibiotics is not difficult or costly. According to Joseph Alton MD fish, antibiotics are essentially the exact same medications as those prescribed by a doctor at a clinic; you just have to know what to look for when you buy.

Setting Up the SHTF Medical Clinic

If you have the medical expertise and feel that it's your duty to help your community or you simply have a large family and or prepper group, then you will need to have supplies on hand that will allow you to set up an SHTF medical clinic.

This need not be elaborate or expensive but you do need to go beyond the items recommend above which are only suitable for a small group or family. You will need the same supplies when setting up an SHTF medical clinic as those for a smaller group; you will just need more of everything to meet the demand.

You will also need a few other items that will be specific to setting up and running a SHTF medical clinic, items such as a large tent, a building or a room inside a building, a number of beds or military cots, stretchers, large amounts of PPE (personal protection equipment), like gloves, face shields, etc.

You could even have a pull trailer or panel truck set up as a mobile SHTF medical clinic that you could drive or pull to wherever you're needed and provide medical care to those in need.

You Medical Library

Below are ten must have medical books for preppers; there are many more that could be included but these are the top ten to start your library with...

1. Where There Is No Doctor: A Village Health Care Handbook, Revised Edition by David Werner and Carol Thuman
2. Where There Is No Dentist by Murray Dickson
3. The Survival Medicine Handbook: A Guide for When Help is not on the Way by Joseph Alton
4. Emergency War Surgery: The Survivalist's Medical Desk Reference by U.S. Army

112

5. Wilderness Medicine: Beyond First Aid by William W. Forgey M.D.
6. The Survival Nurse: Running an Emergency Nursing Station Under Adverse Conditions by Ragnar Benson
7. Prescription for Herbal Healing, 2nd Edition: An Easy-to-Use A-to-Z Reference to Hundreds of Common Disorders and Their Herbal Remedies by Phyllis A. Balch CNC
8. Prescription for Drug Alternatives: All-Natural Options for Better Health without the Side Effects by James F. Balch
9. Medical Diagnosis and Treatment by Maxine Papadakis
10. Where There Is No Psychiatrist: A Mental Health Care Manual by Vikram Patel

Chapter 10

PREPPER COMMUNICATIONS

Prepper communications, those words have stirred confusion in the minds of preppers for years, and after reading many books and magazine articles on that subject over the years, it is easy to see why. Most writings make the subject look far more complicated than it really is, I am not sure if this is intentional to make you think you have to do months of study, and spend thousands of dollars so you can be in the club, or if it's just human tendency to overly complicate things.

However, no matter the reason for previous writers over-complicating the subject, my goal here is to make it as simple, unintimidating, and cheap as possible to get your communications set up properly, so you can stay informed and communicate with your family, group, and outside world.

First we will look at several different readily types of radios for two-way communications. These will include radios to keep in touch with you group in your area as well as to contact others over long distances…

Citizens Band Radio

Anyone in the south who grew up watching The Dukes of Hazard should already be familiar with CB radio and the lingo that goes with it.

This type of radio communications used to be very popular in the U.S. because it was cheap and easy to get set-up, required no tests or licensing and was effective for ranges up to several miles when using mobile units and much farther when using more powerful (and often tuned up) base units, boosters and large antenna arrays.

But nowadays CB radio has fallen out of favor with most people, however, I think this was due more to the cost and service availability of cell phone service, now cell service is available and reliable even in rural areas, and the CB radio can't compete.

Nevertheless, even with all the advancements in other areas of communications, the CB radio still has a place in prepper's communications plan. However, I would not use CB radio as my main method of communications with my group, because in bad times, when cell service might not be available, many people will go back to using CB radio, causing it to become one of the most insecure methods of communications.

Ham Radio

With Ham, radio users can talk over very long distances with the help of repeaters, but to legally transmit you will need to study for, take, and pass a test to get a license. You can listen to all you want without a license, but you cannot legally transmit. Another downside is the fact that the repeater towers may not be in operation in the aftermath of an SHTF event.

However, during a long-term and wide-reaching disaster, the FCC probably will not have the time or resources to track down and prosecute people transmitting via ham radio frequencies.

If you're interested in becoming a "Ham operator" then I recommend, that you start out small at first, this will allow you to "dip your toes in the water" to see how far that you want to go with this hobby before investing a lot of money. A good starter radio is the Baofeng Walkie Talkie UV-5R5, and you will need a good study book, there are several good ones listed at Amazon.com.

GMRS

General Mobile Radio Service (GMRS) are for short-distance two-way communication and requires a license to legally transmit – however the immediate family members of a license holder can also legally use GMRS frequencies to communicate with each other over several miles depending on the terrain.

These radios are sold at electronics stores, department stores like Walmart and Kmart. Most people I know use them without having or worrying about getting a license. The General Mobile Radio Service, like CB radio, will be one of the most used and thus insecure types of two-way communications available.

Having a couple of GMRS radios around is not a bad idea, but as is the case with CB radio I would not make it my primary two-way communications frequency when the SHTF.

FRS

Family Radio Service (FRS) radios have a range of about one mile over good level terrain without obstructions, and the frequencies

116

typically come standard with GMRS two-way radios found in my electronic, sporting goods and department stores. No test or license is required to operate FRS radios in the United States.

The main downside with using the FRS frequencies and radios is again limited range. And the fact that because radios operating within this frequency range are so common that others in your area are sure to be crowding the same frequencies or even hiding nearby and listening in on your conversation to gain intel about what you have and how well manned and armed you and your group are.

List of FRS and GMRS channels

ChannelFrequency (MHz)

- 1   462.5625   Shared with GMRS
- 2   462.5875   Shared with GMRS
- 3   462.6125   Shared with GMRS
- 4   462.6375   Shared with GMRS
- 5   462.6625   Shared with GMRS
- 6   462.6875   Shared with GMRS
- 7   462.7125   Shared with GMRS
- 8   467.5625   FRS use only
- 9   467.5875   FRS use only
- 10   467.6125   FRS use only
- 11   467.6375   FRS use only
- 12   467.6625   FRS use only
- 13   467.6875   FRS use only
- 14   467.7125   FRS use only

Multi-Use Radio Service (MURS)

MURS radios are my preferred choice for two-way communications with two-way hand-held radios because they provide a decent range for communications, no license is required for MURS usage within the United States, and currently few people use them, thus making them more private than the other options mentioned.

MURS is also the same frequency range used with the Dakota driveway alarm and motion sensors, which makes it convenient and cost effective when you use the same radios to communicate with each other and to intrusion warnings on the same frequencies and radios... MURS 2-Way Handheld Radios cost fewer than one hundred bucks on Amazon.com.

Military Field Phones

Military type field phones are the most secure type of communications for preppers, you can have then set up and wired between your main retreat and your LP/OP, workshop or to your neighbor's house for example.

These phones can be found at military surplus dealers or online for around $200 a set and are well worth it if you want to ensure secure communications between two points. I suggest either the TA-312/PT or the TA-1042 field phones, and cable that is rated for underground burial to protect and hide your lines from threats.

News Monitoring

Every household should have at least one AM / FM + Shortwave Receiver to monitor the news from around the world. To get the best signal and sound quality buy the best radio that you can afford. I have two including a Kaito Voyager Pro KA600 and will be adding a third radio, an Eton Grundig Satellit 750 in a few weeks.

When you buy an AM / FM + Shortwave Receiver also pick up one of the rolls up Shortwave antennas to improve reception and go online and do a search for shortwave stations and copy those that you like down, print off and tape one copy up on the wall at your listening post.

Another radio that you will need for monitoring is a police scanner; these will allow you to listen in on police, fire, rescue, and other emergency services in your area. Get one that will run off of off AA batteries as well as standard 110 AC current from you home power outlet... I have used the Uniden Handheld Scanner (BC75XLT) for years and have been very happy with it.

Keeping it all Powered and Running

As you have probably realized all of this communications gear requires some form of power to keep operating, and when you can no longer provide that needed power it all will go silent. Moreover, while nothing lasts forever, our goal is to keep it all running for as long as possible.

To make this possible and to simplify logistics it is a good idea to standardize to one battery size and that should be AA. This battery size is easy to find, cheap to stock up on and small so you can store more units in the same sized space than you could with say, D sized batteries.

Stock up on as many rechargeable AA batteries as you can afford (within reason of course - 50 to 100 would be a good number). Then after you get your battery stockpile squared away, you will need to buy a SunJack 20W Portable Solar Charger and SunJack USB Battery Charger AA/AAA Batteries, get two or three of these for insurance against breakage...

Standardizing with AA sized batteries, having a stockpile of rechargeable AA's and a way to charge those batteries will keep your communications gear powered and operating for years.

This is the first step that every new prepper should take toward using solar power... Once you get you battery stockpile and SunJack solar charger, it is then time to look into setting up more powerful solar arrays and battery banks for more power and capacity.

Start small and grow your solar power options as you can afford to do so. A good second step is the Renogy 200 Watts 12 Volts Monocrystalline Solar Bundle Kit; I have used this kit for over two years with no issues. You can then add more panels to increase output as needed...

One of the best AM/FM + Shortwave radios available for preppers is the Kaito Voyager Pro KA600 that has its own solar panel and crank generator for charging the batteries it will also run off of standard 110 AC current. Every prepper should have two of these – the extra is insurance again breakage.

Chapter 11

Defending Your Home and or Retreat

I've talked to preppers all over the United States and one common trend that I've noticed though those conversations were that many are under the impression that after just about any type of disaster that they will be able to defend their homes and/or retreats with unaccounted for deadly force via the barrel of a gun.

From those conversations, it is also easy to see that they are under the false impression that a disaster of the magnitude of an economic collapse, also will result in a full collapse of the government and any rule of law and accountability for their actions.

Where they got this info is beyond me, because common sense or history does not support their beliefs. Perhaps they've watched too many doomsday type movies or read one too many "prepper novels", but the fact is that the federal government has spent billions of taxpayer dollars on their own preps and have contingency plans in place that will allow them to stay in power after just about any type of disaster imaginable.

Granted their power may be significantly reduced or even nonexistent in some areas perhaps for months or even years, but the federal government isn't going to just go away or disappear altogether, in fact, I expect the exact opposite.

They have already enacted laws that will allow the federal government to declare martial law with the stroke and drying ink of the presidential pen. No, the federal government is not going to go away after an economic collapse or any other likely disaster, but instead will clamp down via the declaration of martial law.

This will be especially evident in the larger cities and urban areas. Those areas may be cordoned to prevent rioting from spilling out past a certain point, but after the looting and burning subside, probably in about three or five days when the food supplies run out, troops will move in and take control of those locations via force and a declaration of martial law.

Nevertheless, one thing is certain and that is that the federal government, even with the help of state and local National Guard and police does not have the manpower to control the entire geographic area of the United States at once. This is the reason they will concentrate their resources and manpower toward controlling the cities and urban areas that we talked about a minute ago.

After a major disaster, there very well may be a period without the rule of law (WROL), out in the rural areas this could last for weeks, months or perceivably even years. However, unlike what has been seen in the pages of countless survival fiction books and movies, it will most likely be a short-term event, especially in the cities.

You see most people want law and order and will work together to achieve that end. Crime will no doubt increase, after an economic collapse (and after most other disasters), with home invasions, robbery, murder, kidnapping and rape being all too common, but such offenses will still be against the law, both legally and morally, and people will demand that the perpetrators are apprehended and justice served.

This is where the majority of preppers seem to be confused (and trigger-happy). We have all heard, read, and contemplated it but is the shoot-first-crowd being realistic or simply feeding their Rambo fantasies with visions of using uncontrolled, and unaccounted-for deadly force on their neighbors or anyone else that comes within one thousand yards of their retreat after the balloon goes up…

Listen; in all but the most extreme circumstances of total and long-term collapse and anarchy (example = full blown civil war), the laws, and punishment for the unjustifiable taking of a human life will still apply, and will be enforced, even if that punishment is your public execution in the street. You will not be able to kill your neighbor because he looked at your wife with lust in his eyes, or trespassed on your property without there being repercussions brought against you.

My advice is to study up on the laws regarding self-defense in your state and to also have non-lethal means of protecting yourself, such as defensive spray, extendable baton, Taser, bean bag rounds etc.... You see, having lethal and non-lethal means of defending yourself and your home and/or retreat gives you options that you can employ depending of the situation.

Granted; you may have to use deadly force to protect yourself and your family, but be sure that it is justifiable by law and moral standards before you pull the trigger. To do otherwise may result in your being thrown into jail or worse, leaving your family without you and in a much more vulnerable position.

It is a good idea to be friends with your local Sheriff and as many of his deputies as possible - remember they write the reports (just hope that it was not one of their family or friends that you shot).

A good shovel and bag of hydrated lime might also be a good idea, you know, just in case that you let things get out of hand...

Those that use unjustifiable lethal force against another person will be held accountable if caught, no matter how bad the disaster or how deep and far reaching the crash it maybe. To think otherwise is a sure way of ending up in jail or worse.

Keeping that reality in mind is what sets this chapter apart from most of the other information written on the same subject and repeated within the prepper community.

OCOKA

OCOKA is a military term that stands for – Observation and fields of fire, Cover, and Concealment, Obstacles, Key Terrain, Avenues of Approach. When setting up retreat and home defenses OCOKA should always be kept in mind and each principle addressed. Following these five key principles, you will greatly improve your security and survivability. Let us take a quick look at each in more detail.

Observation and Fields of Fire

You need to be able to see a potential threat at the earliest opportunity if you can see the threat early, and hopefully, before that threat can see you, then you can make the correct decisions to either make contact, hide, or prepare to defend your area with force.

Can you observe all avenues of approach from your retreat? Do you have a full 360 degrees of view around your property? Are there areas that intruders could exploit to get close and possibly steal from, loot or attack you without being seen?

If forced could you fire upon an attacker from all angles without them being able to hide from view or without you possibly accidentally, shooting your neighbors or damaging key resources? If not then you need to get to work clearing obstacles that limit your view and ability to fire upon an attacker if you are forced to do so.

Cover and Concealment

Cover is protection from bullets and concealment is something you can hide behind where an attacker cannot see you, but concealment offers no protection from gunfire. No matter what you've seen in the movies, car doors, kitchen tables, typical home entry doors, or the bed mattress isn't cover and will not reliably protect you from being struck by bullets as they pass through.

If there is not any natural cover at your retreat, then you will need to get to work now constructing something that will protect you from bullets. You could build some decorative concrete or rock walls, tall raised flower or garden beds. These could provide effective cover, and still allow your home to blend in with other homes around you and not look like a fortification.

It is also a good idea to have a supply of sandbags on hand that can be filled with sand and/or dirt to provide an effective way to put up cover quickly in needed areas. Even unused trashcans that are filled with sand or dirt can work well if you have several to work with. Just remember that the area between the cans does not provide effective cover, only concealment, no matter how closely that you push them together.

Obstacles

Obstacles are used to slow or stop an attacker or to force him to go in a different direction either away from you or into a position where he is more vulnerable to you; preferably, into an area that offers him no means of cover or concealment.

One of the simplest and effective obstacles that you can put up is a fence. Do not wait until a disaster; get to work putting up a fence now. It will increase your security and probably, your property value. The key, to success here is to take a look around at the other houses in your area and note what types of fencing is already in use and put up a similar type around your property. The key is to blend in with everyone else; this will help you to avoid becoming a target.

Obstacles can also be used to stop vehicles from entering your property or neighborhood. For example felling several trees closely together in an interwoven pattern can be a very effective obstacle that can even stop tracked vehicles if done correctly.

No matter how strong the obstacles that you put in place are given enough time an attacker can work through and remove that obstacle if given enough time by being unchallenged. Key areas and avenues of approach should be blocked by obstacles, and covered by observation. This will give you and your group early warning and time to escape or mount an offensive attack against the trespassers.

Key Terrain

Key Terrain is any piece of terrain that offers an advantage to whoever controls it. Think the high ground. If you can take the high ground it can drastically increase your observation, and offer an advantage if your area comes under attack. Take control of and retain that key terrain, you do not want a potential attacker to gain control of that area and be able to use it to watch you or worse use it to attack you or your area. One lone sniper could use the advantage given by such key terrain to wipe out your entire family, group or community, with a few well-placed rifle shots.

Even if you are in an urban area or the ground for miles under your feel is flat any taller than normal buildings can be viewed as key terrain or the high ground. Control these and use them to your advantage.

Avenues of Approach

This goes hand-in-hand with observation and fields of fire – look around and note the most likely avenues of approach that an

126

intruder or attacker would take to reach you. Watch roads, pathways, waterways and open areas that lead up to your property, key terrain as mentioned above will offer a huge advantage here. And remember the father you can see the threat the better, distance will give you more time to decide what needs to be done and how to do it, depending on the threat presented.

OKOKA – observation, fields of fire, cover and concealment, obstacles, key terrain, and avenues of approach. Memorize it and use it when setting up your home and retreat defenses.

Now let us look at a few additional but key defensive strategies to keep in mind...

Stay Hidden

No doubt about it; the surest way to survive a fight is to avoid getting into one in the first place. Too many preppers have an offensive mindset when it comes to retreat defense. Sadly, many will suffer for it. Forget about the macho bullshit, there is no shame in hiding until a threat passes by, in fact, it is the smart thing to do.

As a family or small survival group, you cannot afford to risk injuries or worse casualties because you let your ego driven Rambo fantasies to guide you into taking offensive action when it could have been avoided it. However, you should be ready to violently, defend your area and retreat if a confrontation cannot be avoided.

Combat Multipliers

A combat multiplier is anything that makes you and your group more effective or more difficult for an attacker to defeat. You should amass as many combat multipliers as possible now, before the time of need. You do not want to wait until the marauders are coming through the window to start thinking about it, then it will be too late. Do not put off until tomorrow what should be done today, your life depends on it.

Things like knowing your terrain, improvised alarms, holding key terrain, having long-range weapons, night vision equipment, body armor, two-way radios, semi-automatic weapons, putting in obstacles or reinforcing natural ones, camouflage, mobility, trained guard dogs etc. are all combat multipliers and should be considered in your retreat defensive plans.

Funneling the Attack

Funneling the attack in the simplest terms means using obstacles (both natural and manmade) to "guide the attacker(s) into a place of your choosing and where you have a definitive tactical advantage.

Ambush and the Element of Surprise

An ambush can be used as both an offensive and defensive tactical maneuver, for example, an ambush could be used to attack a convoy in an offensive maneuver outside of your perimeter, and to defend against an attacker or attackers, that have entered your property or home. Hide and wait until the attackers have reached a predetermined position where they are most vulnerable, then spring the ambush.

An effective ambush does not always mean shooting and killing those being ambushed, while gunfire is an option depending on the circumstances, you can us an ambush to capture potential attackers and then make a decision on what to do with them after you have gained more knowledge through questioning or interrogation.

Early Warning is Necessary

The sooner you know an intrusion is going to happen the better, time will allow you and your group to make a decision to stay and

128

fight or make a speedy get-a-way. If you decide to stay and fight, early warning will hopefully, allow you the time to get into the best possible defendable position, or to plan an effective ambush.

Early warning for trespassers or attackers can come from a number of different options. For example; informants, lookouts placed in key locations that lead up to your retreat, dogs, motion activated lights, improved alarms, spot lights, security cameras etc.

It is best not to rely on just one type of early warning device because it might be bypassed, or could fail. For example, you could have a look out a mile or two away with a two-way radio overlooking a road or trail that leads into your location, then improvised alarm devices a little further in, and then guard dogs on the outskirts and perimeter of your property or retreat location.

Layered Defense

You should divide your area into three layers of defense – the outer layer, intermediate layer, and the inner layer. The outer layer could be the area as far as you can see out past your property line, the intermediate layer could be anywhere inside your property line and the inner layer would be your home. With each layer, providing increasing levels of security and protection.

You need to have a plan of action for each layer of your defense grid. For example, your outer layer could be a watch and report area only with no action taken against anyone that wonders inside that layer. Unless, of course, you know that they are planning to attack and loot you at your location, then defensive action should be taken to prevent them from ever reaching your second or third layer of defense.

Your second layer would probably be your property line; a chained link or barbed wire fence would preferably mark this layer boundary. Anyone crossing into this area is probably up to no good and should be dealt with quickly, and aggressively; the extent of your aggression will depend on the depth and length of the disaster and the threat posed by the aggressors.

Your third layer would be inside your home and in most cases deadly force can and should be used here.

The key to an effective layered defense is for you and your group to know where each layer begins and ends and to have a predetermined plan of action for each layer when that layer has been breached, and to practice each scenario until it can be done effectively, even when you are tired and hungry.

Misinformation

Misinformation is simply, leading anyone your group to believe something that you want them to believe that is not true. Let us say for example that you know or suspect that someone or a group is listening in on your two-way radio communications, to gain Intel before they loot or steal from you. You can use this fact to your advantage, by feeding them false information via your two-way communications or through know informants.

For example; you could make them believe that your group is larger or better armed than you are or lead them to think you are going to be in one place but in reality, you are setting an ambush, or planning your escape. The key is to make it believable and have a workable plan where you can use their response to your false information to your tactical advantage.

False or misleading information could be used to make your neighbors think that you are worse off than they are. For example, you could show up at their door begging for food, when in fact you have a well-stocked pantry. Just do not be too aggressive by demanding that they share whatever they have with you because, you might get shot if they mistake you as a threat.

Official looking signs can also be used to good effect when planting seeds of false information, for example; you could post official looking "Food and Water 5 Miles" with an arrow pointing down the road and away from your location. Use your imagination and I am sure that you can come up with other ideas for signs that will mislead and confuse strangers that wander into your town or onto your property.

Defensive Positions

Most homes are not built to defeat gunfire and bullets will pass right through the walls and riddle anyone caught in between. It is best to defend your home from the outside where you have more visibility and mobility. This is where your early warning devices come into play, by knowing when someone is approaching your location, even before they get there, will allow you and your group time to get into a defensive or ambush position.

Sandbags are very useful and effective when setting up defensive poisons that offer ballistic cover. They are cheap enough (or can be improvised) that you can stock up on hundreds of bags for under $100 and can be filled with sand or dirt that you dig up from your property.

Although; you do not want to defend your home from the inside, it is still a good idea to build up the area around and near the windows with filled sandbags. This will offer cover if for some unfortunate reason you were surprised and trapped inside the structure.

Lining the area inside your pouch up to the railing with filled sandbags is also a good idea. This will offer a protected shooting position that can be occupied quickly if an attacker or trespasser were to get inside your second layer of defense before you have time to staff your main defensive positions away from your main living structure.

Your main defensive positions should be set up in key locations around your property and can range from hardened pillbox type structures with thick reinforced concrete or rammed earth walls to simple spider holes, or a mixture of both.

Do Not Look Like an Easy Target

Do not be an easy target, and even if you are, you can use misinformation to make would be looters or attackers think that you are far stronger and better armed than you really are. If they think you are a hard target hopefully, they will think that going up against you is not worth the risk and move on in search of an easier target.

OPSEC – Operational Security

We hear this all of the time in prepper and survivalist circles, OPSEC aka operational security and it is very important now and will be a major factor toward keeping you and your group secure after the balloon goes up. The number one rule of OPSEC is to keep your mouth shut – everything should be done on a need-to-know basis and most people do not need to know anything about what you and your group are doing.

A Plan of Retreat

No matter how well prepared or strong our defenses, we could be faced with a superior force that greatly outnumber and outgun us, where staying and fighting would be suicidal. You need a plan of retreat, preferably, a way to retreat without being seen or confronted by the superior force. An escape tunnel from your home that leads to a hidden and safe evacuation point would be an ideal. However, most preppers do not have the room or the resources to put such a plan and tunnels into place.

Again, this is where early two-way-radio warning lookouts and alarms can save your life. If you know a threat is approaching you, have time to evaluate the threat and make a decision of whether to stay and fight or retreat. You should have a predetermined destination where everyone in your group knows to meet up if you are forced from your retreat area.

Also having caches of first aid, water, food and ammo along the way and at the safe location is a good idea. Get those into place now, before the time of need. In addition, each member of your group should have an escape or "bug out bag" that can be quickly grabbed as the escape plan is being put into action.

I know many preppers will resist the thought of retreating from their retreat, preferring to stay and fight even if defeat and death are certain. You know; take out as many of those SOB's as possible before they take your location and while this is admirable, it is not always the best decision.

The escape can be used to buy you time to get better organized, and plan for a counter attack where you can ultimately, take your property back from the aggressors. I have talked to several preppers who have their main food caches hidden on their property while having a separate smaller cache out in the open for looters to find if they make it that far.

However, the surprise is that those preppers have poisoned that "decoy cache" of food items. Therefore, they plan to retreat, wait, then come back and remove the looters / attackers after they have died of the poison. While this plan is not the most moral course of action, it is effective.

Chapter 12

SELF-SUFFICIENCY: THE KEY TO LONG-TERM SURVIVAL

Face reality, unless you are super rich putting back more than six months to a one-year food supply, isn't practical, and even if you have the cash to spend, finding room for storage and the constant dating and rotating become the next obstacle, and this can get quickly become unmanageable.

For most preppers the goal should be a one-year food storage reserve, this should see you through most disasters, but you should also plan and work toward becoming as self-reliant as possible where you are. If you can grow and forage for all or most of your own food then you can survive for decades if need be, and eat healthier too.

In this chapter, I will cover some key points learned from my experience running a small homestead and providing most of my own food for over a decade. This includes gardening, foraging, and raising domestic livestock as well as tips on preserving the bounty of your work.

Self-Sufficiency Starts with the Survival Workshop

The ability to use tools has been a major contributing factor to our survival and growth as a species, but unfortunately, that ability has turned into a specialty skill set in our increasingly dumbed-down, in the call, "the guy" for everything that needs fixing in the world that we now live in. Unfortunately, for some calling "the guy" may not be an option during a long-term disaster.

You will be "the guy" and if it breaks you will probably be the one who has to fix it, and aside from the obvious of needing to know what you are doing, you will also need the correct tools to do the job effectively.

Nothing beats hands-on learning and experience, and you can get that by signing up for any courses available in your area. Look into welding, woodworking, auto mechanics etc. learn all you can, because skills will be needed for your own use and well as being an excellent barter item that no one can steal from you.

You can often get free training, by offering your help to local businesses that specialize in the skills that you want to learn. Tell them that you would like to offer your help free in exchange for them helping you learn those skills. As long as they know that, you are not trying to learn, so that you can then set up as competition later, most will welcome the offer.

As for what tools you will need that really depends on your skills in using those tools, once you gain skills you will know also know

what tools you need in your toolbox. But not matter what tool you buy always buy the very best quality that you can afford – low-quality tools often break during use and cause all kinds of cursing, disappointment, and unfinished work.

Another thing to keep in mind when selecting and buying tools is that power from the utility might not be available, therefore hand tools that run on muscle power and sweat should be given top priority, in the prepper's tool box, and then rechargeable tools that

can be charged via solar or generator power.

The Prepper's Garden

When it comes to gardening everyone seems to have their own ideas as to what is "the best" method, and they all could be right, because different methods are required for different situations and locations, but never the less the basics are still the same. You start with a seed, seedling, or cutting, plant it, nurture it, harvest it, and eventually eat it. Generally, you will need a fertile soil with a pH-balanced level of between 6.5. - 7, well drained, with six or more hours of direct sunlight, and fresh water to grow a healthy, productive garden. If you can provide this type of growing environment, then the plants will do well without much else from you.

With the survival garden, you goal should be to grow as much produce as possible, on the least space as possible, while doing the least amount of work as possible. Remember minimum effort and the maximum reward is the goal, because if you burn more calories planting and tending your garden than you get back from the harvest, you then have a negative return for your effort, which goes again the rules of human survival.

I have found a mix of close planting (sometimes called French intensive) and Ruth Stout's method as detailed in her book gardening without work, works very well for me, producing an abundant harvest with little effort on my part.

With Ruth Stout's gardening method you simply keep a thick layer of mulch (usually hay, straw or leaves) on the garden at all times, this keeps down weeds and automatically builds the soil and adds nutrients back as it decays. As it decays into the soil, you simply add more mulch, keeping it at a consistent level to keep smoother weed growth.

There is no need to build and turn a compost pile, or plow, sow a cover crop, weed, and seldom have to water, or do anything else besides adding mulch and plants to grow a productive garden.

The only fertilizers that I use are manure tea, cottonseed, or soybean meal, and then only need small amounts these, especially after the first couple of years once the soil has time to become fertile from constantly rotting mulch.

To plant you simply pull back the mulch and plant the seeds, cutting or seedlings as you normally would in any garden. And that that there is to it, mulch, plant, let grow, rest, harvest.

Guerrilla Gardening

Guerrilla gardening is a term used by local pot farmers, who have developed unique skills that allow them to raise the "illegal plants" in a secretive manner. However, before you get all excited with visions of easy money and smoke puffing from a freshly rolled marijuana cigarette, let me clear the smoke from the air, this article is not about growing the illegal weed; it is about growing secret food crops after a complete breakdown of the current system and WROL.

Having the traditional garden planted in rolls and in the open could make you the target of looters, scavengers, and thugs. Having your garden hidden and out of site could mean the difference between plenty and starvation after the balloon goes up.

Secret Grow Rooms

Secret grow rooms or greenhouses should be considered, all that is needed in most cases is to remove the roof from a garage or outbuilding and replace it with corrugated fiberglass. The walls can be painted white, or covered with aluminum foil, to help reflect light back onto the plants inside. From the outside, it just looks like any other outbuilding, while inside it hides an abundant garden.

Tables for plants can be made and rigged on pulleys, so the plants can be lifted closer to the roof providing more sunlight and lowered back down again for watering. Using this method, it would be difficult to grow enough to feed an entire family, but it could be done with proper planning and enough space. Most likely, the secret grow-room would be used to supplement other available food resources.

Order a copy of – Secret Greenhouse of Survival: How to Build the Ultimate Homestead & Prepper Greenhouse by Rick Austin for a full plan on setting up a secret greenhouse.

Forest Gardens

Many people have mentioned forest gardens; the idea has been around for a long time, and could work well, for the survivor or a person bugging out to the forest. All you do is – find a suitable spot that is hidden, well drained, and open to sunlight. Dig up the soil, work in organic matter, or timed released fertilizers and plant.

If done right, such a garden can be largely self-maintaining requiring little effort by you after planting.

Avoid making trails to the garden area, people follow trails, and these will lead them directly to your garden, remember the harder it is for you to reach the gardens location the more likely no one else will even try.

Remove all signs of activity, like trash or freshly dug soil. Spread any loose dirt over the area covering any open spots with natural ground cover such as leaves. This also helps form mulch reducing the need for watering significantly. Try to make the garden area blend in with the surrounding forest as much as possible.

Step back and look at the possible approach points, and remove anything that catches the eye. Remember to avoid making trails to and from the site by never going in or out the same way and using alternating entry points. Try to walk on hard surfaces as much as possible to avoid leaving tracks.

Blending In

Some plants are easier to hide than others are; potatoes, for instance, would be easier to hide than say tomatoes or corn. Most people would pass within three feet of a potato patch and not recognize what they were looking at. Choosing plants that blend in with the surrounding is an important consideration for the secret survival gardener.

The Gardening Nomad

I know a guy who lived in a truck camper for years - he would move from one hide to another every couple of weeks, he had gardens strategically located all over the countryside. I do not know if they were all legal crops (probably not), but know that some of what he grew what he grew were food crops and he seemed to do very well, while living a very simple life, all without a lot of stress and worry.

Three Sisters of the Cherokee

Another growing technique that I recommend is "the three sisters". This system has been used for thousands of years with great success in both North and South America by many "Indian" tribes and native people.

The three sisters consist of corn, squash, and beans that are planted in a circle, with corn in the center, then pole beans are then planted around the corn and then squash are planted around the outside. The pole beans help to put nitrogen back into the soil, which is great for the corn and squash. The beans climb up the corn, which acts as a natural trellis. The squash with its wide leaves help shade out weeds and reduces the need for watering. It all works together in a sort of mini garden ecosystem.

Perennials

Perennials are my secret weapon against post-collapse hunger pains and starvation - planting perennials will allow you to have a continually replicating food supply, which will provide for you year after year with little effort on your part. Every prepper should establish a good variety of perennial edibles at their retreat.

I have established "gardens" of asparagus, Jerusalem artichokes, horseradish, garlic, perennial onions, and herbs scattered around my homestead. Once these perennials are planted, and established, they continue to grow and expand every year on their own with little or no help from you...

Choosing Seeds

At the beginning of the growing season most gardeners, simply head to their nearest garden center, and pick up whatever seed packets that are being displayed on the shelf that year, or they skip the seeds and their germination altogether by purchasing seedlings and transplanting those directly into their garden.

And why this works well (sometimes) during "good times" when you can still rely on going back and getting new seed for planting a new crop each year, if you're thinking in terms of long-term survival or saving your own seed from year to year, then you need to consider buying and stockpiling Non-Hybrid (Heirloom) vegetable seeds.

According to the good folks at Heirloom Organics:

> *Non-Hybrid or Open-Pollinated seeds allow the gardener to collect seeds from a crop for future planting. Hybrid seeds do not. Heirloom Organics Seed Packs are 100% Non-Hybrid and Non-GMO (genetically modified) and specially sealed for long-term storage. Use now AND save for an emergency. All from the same hermetically sealed pack!*

And while this is true in most cases, saving seed from year-to-year that grows true, without negative genetic changes is a little more complicated than that. Some plant species, such as corn, okra, and spinach, for example, must "cross-pollinate" each year to remain strong and to be productive.

Constant inbreeding of cross-pollinating plans, even if they are of the non-hybrid variety will result in weak, non-productive plans after the first couple of years. Therefore, even if you start with pure non-hybrid, heirloom seed you cannot save the seed of cross-pollinating species, indefinitely without a negative change in the resulting offspring at some point, due to inbreeding of the plants.

The solution to this problem is to simply, buy enough seed to last several years, and stored in optimal conditions to ensure germination, or buy several different Non-Hybrid, Non-GMO varieties and cross-pollinate each year.

Now the good news, self-pollinating plant species such as bean, pepper, tomato, eggplant, garlic, and pea can be grown and the seeds saved year-after-year with little or no genetic change in growth, health, or overall production, allowing you to continually feed your family, now and during hard times.

Over the years, I have seen many folks express concerns about the germination rate of seeds that have been packaged for long-term storage, such as the Non-Hybrid vegetable seeds that are packaged and sold by Heirloom Organics and other seed vendors.

The main concern seems to be that the process and conditions of storing the seed long-term will somehow cause the seed to not germinate (sprout) when planted. After having tested these seeds and their germination rates over the past several years, and others have done the same with similar results, I can assure you that germination rates remain just as good as or better than seeds stored in a traditional fashion.

Putting back a supply of non-hybrid vegetable seed should be on the to-do-list of every, gardener and that applies ten-fold for the "prepper" because we do not know what will happen, the result or how long the duration. We can only store so much food, and after it is gone, you will have to produce your own or starve.

142

Fruits, Nuts, and Berries

Fruits, nuts, and berries are one of my favorite hedges against starvation because they can be planted once and then mostly take care of themselves after. However, the biggest benefit is that after planted and established they will come back and provide for years after without you having to do much in the way of care… Plant it and forget it… well almost.

If you have an empty space on your property, then fill that space by planting a food bearing tree, vine, or shrub. To fill larger areas plant fruit and nut trees, and for smaller areas consider planting strawberries, raspberries, rhubarb, blueberries etc. No space should be left empty especially around a small homestead…

Let us start with fruit trees, since these tend to produce the most food for the least amount of work. When choosing fruit trees, look either dwarf or semi-dwarf varieties depending on the space you have available. Never plant a dwarf tree if you have room for a semi-dwarf variety, the semi-dwarf trees grow to a larger size and thus they will produce more fruit under the same growing conditions, they are also more winter hardy, and live longer.

It's also a good idea to plant a variety of different trees, shrubs and vines that produce different types of fruit, nuts and berries, i.e. apple, pear, peach, plum, cherry, blackberry, blueberry, raspberry etc. This will not only provide you with more variety at the table, it will also act as insurance against pest and disease that might attack one variety or plant but not another.

Also, when planting apple trees, I suggest that you plant both summer and winter varieties, as you might have assumed summer varieties mature and are ready for harvest before the winter varieties which makes it easier to harvest and preserve the fruit because it's not all ready for harvest all at once.

As for planting instructions, I am not going to get into that here simply because the details can vary slightly depending on location and type. You will find that the planting instructions for your location will come with the trees, shrubs and vines when you buy them at the nursery, if not ask.

When choosing varieties for cross-pollination, you can use the free tool at www.orangepippintrees.com/pollinationchecker.aspx to help you make the correct choices. Also, ask at the nursery when you buy your fruit trees for their advice on pollination and their recommendations.

I recommend that before planting your first tree, shrub or vine that you order a copy of The Fruit Gardener's Bible: A Complete Guide to Growing Fruits and Nuts in the Home Garden by Lewis Hill this is a great book that is dedicated to the subject, and will cover everything that you need to know and then some.

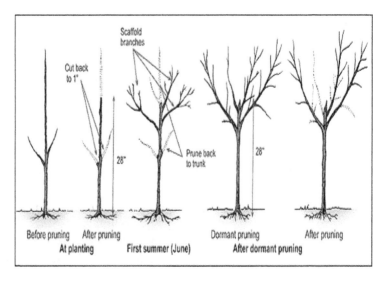

Fruit Tree Pruning Instructions – dormant pruning is done in late fall or winter when the leaves have fallen off.

Practical Domestic Animals and Poultry for Preppers

When choosing which domestic animals to keep for food, look for those that require the least time and effort to care for. As I explained in the gardening section above, when surviving, you do not want to put in more effort, and thus, burn more calories, then you are going to get back upon consumption.

Look for animals that can generally take care of themselves, like with anything else that you do when trying to survive look for the most reward for the least effort. For example, you do not want to exert 1000 calories, searching for an egg that you are only going to get 78 calories from. If you do this for consistently, then you are ensuring a slow withering death from malnutrition...

Chickens

No section on raising domestic animals for food would be complete without taking a closer look at raising chickens. Chickens are usually the first thought that pops into a person's head when they think about farming or homesteading and for good reason.

Really the only downside to raising chickens is the initial startup costs of having to build a coop and feeders and watering containers, after that the cost per bird is extremely low, especially if your let them free-range so that they can forage for most of their own food.

Your main concern will be keeping them safe from predators because everything loves to eat chicken, including but not limited to foxes, raccoons, coyotes, bobcats, mountain lions, owls, hawks, domestic dogs, domestic cats and everything else that likes to eat meat. The best way to keep them safe is to keep

them inside a well-made coop with a securely fenced in outside run, but this means that you'll have to feed them more because they generally won't be able to forage for the bulk of their food when confined to such a limited space.

As a compromise, I keep my chickens inside the coop with access to the eight by twenty-five foot run most of the day and let them out to forage of the evenings about two hours before dark. They generally stay within seventy-five yards of the coop, and will go back in to roost before dark. After they are all in I'll go lock the door to the coop, to keep any predators out and the chickens' safe inside.

When building your coop seal any openings uptight, even a small hole can give a hungry predator a way in – some will even use a small opening as a starting point that they can enlarge by chewing until they can squeeze inside.

When building your run, you will want to use treated wood for longevity, and to dig a trench six or more inches deep to bury that length of the wire in the ground to prevent predators from digging in under the fencing. I also like to pile rocks all the way around the coop and run – so far, this has worked great and I have never had a predator that has gotten inside the coop or run by digging.

Another thing to keep in mind is that chicken wire by itself is weak, and will not keep a large determined predator out. When I built my first chicken coop and run, I had two stray dogs that managed to rip through the chicken wire and into the coop. Luckily, I was at home and stopped them before they were able to do any more damage.

After that incident, I have always re-enforced the bottom three feet of chicken wire around the run by covering it with welded-wire. This has been very effective at keeping larger predators out and the chickens' safe inside.

My coop is almost finished in the photo above.

Having an outside dog (one that will not kill chickens) is also a great help at keeping you flock safe and for security in general. A good dog will keep watch and run predators off when they wonder into the area before they have a chance to find their way into your coop.

When choosing a type of chicken for survival purposes, look for dual-purpose breeds that are both good egg layers and meat producers. You will also want to choose breeds that go broody and that are good mothers so that you can raise additional birds to replace those that are eaten.

Note: hens will continue to lay eggs, even without a rooster but those eggs will not be fertile and with not hatch producing offspring.

My five most recommended breeds for preppers are the Black Australorp, Rhode Island Red, Dominique, Plymouth Rock, and Wyandotte. These breeds meet all of the criteria listed above and are easy to find or order in most areas and easy to care for.

When you start raising chickens, you will find that it is easy to be carried away with the result being that you end up with more birds than you need. For most preppers, a flock consisting of ten hens and two roosters works out well. The extra rooster acts as a "backup" should something happen to the other, allowing your hens to keep producing offspring.

You can find a wealth of free information detailing everything that you could possibly want to know about raising chickens, breeding, medical issues, coop building etc. However, to be honest, it is not that hard and if it is then you are doing it wrong. Remember look for a maximum reward for the least effort, once you get your coop built it should only take about ten minutes per day to take care of your flock.

Ducks

I used to keep a few ducks around, and plan to add ten or more back into my flock this coming spring when I can buy day old ducklings from the local Tractor Supply or Farmers CO-OP, and eventually, I may completely replace my flock of chickens with ducks.

Ducks are smarter than chickens and are better foragers that can find most of their own food, and they are less disease prone and seem to attract fewer predators. Ducks lay just as many eggs as chickens, but the eggs taste better and are larger. They are also better mothers to their young.

Many preppers make the mistake of thinking that they must have a large pond or another body of water on their property to keep ducks, and while the ducks do enjoy that setting, it is not necessary. All that I ever used were several "kiddie pools" that I kept full of water around my property and the ducks thrived.

Since ducks like to poop in the water, you will need to pour it out every week or so and replace it with fresh water. The water from the pools makes an excellent fertilizer that can be poured around your fruit and nut trees.

Rabbits

If the goal is to put meat on the table then you should start building your rabbit hutches now. Rabbits meet or exceed all of the criteria that I previously mentioned about choosing animals that easy to keep and cheap to feed because they do well on nothing more than, fresh dry grass clippings, hay, unused produce from the garden, salt, and fresh water.

I also like to add a hand full of commercial feed pellets for each rabbit every couple of day to round out their diet. This becomes more important during the winter months when fresh grass clippings and hay are not as readily available.

Housing for rabbits is a simple matter; all they need is protection from predators and from harsh weather conditions. Do a web search and you will find a wealth of free hutch building plans, these range from basic but functional to major projects costing several hundred dollars. My preference is to keep it simple and cheap.

You will have to keep the male "buck" separate from the females until you are ready for them to breed. After the female has been breed, remove the male and put him back in his cage. Females are usually ready to breed at around ten months old and will usually bear from eight to fourteen young after a short thirty-day gestation period.

The offspring can be slaughtered after nine weeks and the doe then rebreed again. As you can see if you do the math, one buck and five does can produce a lot of meat quickly. Just don't make the mistake of eating only rabbit meat - rabbit meat is too lean and humans need some fat to survive and a diet consisting of only rabbit meat by itself does not provide enough fat to keep a human body healthy over the long-term.

Larger Animals

If you have enough land to provide the bulk of food and space for larger domestic animals like hogs and cows, then these can prove a huge benefit and should be considered. These larger animals can provide hundreds of pounds of meat, or as is the case with the cow can also provide milk, cheese, and related products as well as meat when slaughtered.

Goats are a great alternative to the cows and are much easier to care for and will find most of the own food if left free to forage over a large enough area. However, keep in mind that they can kill trees, and native foliage, and will eat your garden, flowerbed or just about anything else that they are allowed to get into.

Since this is not a dedicated book on how to care for and harvest domestic animals, I am going to suggest that you order two books – Barnyard in Your Backyard: A Beginner's Guide to Raising Chickens, Ducks, Geese, Rabbits, Goats, Sheep, and Cattle by Gail Damerow and Basic Butchering of Livestock & Game by John J. Mettler. These two books will cover everything that you need to know to successfully raise and butcher domestic livestock and poultry.

Bees and Honey

Honeybees have been vanishing at an alarming rate, with losses of upwards of 40% of bee colonies worldwide over the past few years. In addition, while no one seems to agree on the cause, we can all agree that the loss of our honeybees will throw our ecosystem out of balance, making it more difficult or impossible to grow enough food to support the earth's current population.

Personally, I believe that the predominant cause of this hive die off is due to the increased planting of GMO crops and especially the use of chemical pesticides that the bees carry back to the hive, causing death and eventual hive collapse.

Having one or two beehives can produce 25 to 50 pounds of honey per year if the hive is healthy and well managed. If you want to keep a hive or two at your homestead, the first thing that you should do is to go talk to a local beekeeper that already has established hives. These experienced bee keeps can give you some great pointers on keeping bees in your area and the dangers to look out for, and possibly sell you everything that you need to get started.

Foraging

Foraging for wild foods via hunting, fishing, trapping, and gathering of edible plants and nuts can go a long way toward ensuring your survival after the balloon goes up if you are prepared and have the needed skills to do so. You need to learn how to hunt, trap, and fish as well as how to recognize and prepare the edible plants and nuts that are abundant in your area.

Granted it's impossible to teach someone to hunt by writing about it in a book, you need to get out and do it to learn, but you can pick up a few tips and some how-to-do-it knowledge from reading and watching other people hunt on the Outdoor channel.

Generally, trapping is more efficient than hunting especially for those just starting out; traps can be set and work without you having to be there. Set it, leave it, come back, and check it once a day to remove caught game, rebait the trap or both. You can use the free time to do other needed chores like tending your garden or setting more traps.

Harvesting wild game for the stewpot is excellent long-term survival strategy as long as you do not plan to live off harvested wild game exclusively. Wild game should be considered as only one link, in your food resupply chain, and not as the whole chain.

You must have variable and independent sources of resupply, lined up and ready to go. I have seen too many preppers, who plan to rely 100% on their stored foods. They have no resupply chain, and if the crisis lasts longer than their food stockpile, then they are out of luck.

Plus your stockpile might be looted, burnt, blown away or destroyed a hundred other ways, so please don't put all of your eggs in one basket, so to speak. Plan on losing your main food supply, and make plans that will allow you to keep on feeding your family, regardless of how empty your storage shelves become.

To start, you will need to learn the basics of setting both store bought and homemade traps. To help you in both areas, I suggest that you order copies of The New Buckshot's Complete Survival Trapping Guide by Bruce Hemming, Survival Poaching by Ragnar

Benson and The Modern Hunter-Gatherer: A Practical Guide to Living off the Land by Tony Nester.

However you'll still need to get up and off of your rear-end and actually go outside, and do it. You will need to practice, practice and then practice some more because most animals are smarter than the average human trying to trap them is.

There are other good how-to-do-it trapping books available, but the three are my top recommendations. Just do not think that you are an expert or proficient trapper just because you read a book, you are not.

You have to get outside and DO IT!

As for trap and gear recommendations, I suggest that you lay in a good supply of small game snares, you can make your own snares, but I've found that it's just as cost effective to order them pre-made in bulk than to make your own, especially when you consider your time.

The Dakota line Rabbit Snares are the perfect size and weight for trapping small game like rabbit, squirrel, and pheasant. Larger game can also be taken (easily I might add) with snares, but you will have to make your own, heavyweight snares for this (**disclaimer**: check and follow game laws... yadda, yadda, yadda), full details are given in the pages of Survival Poaching, that I linked to above.

My next trap recommendation is the 110 Single Spring Body Trap, these are perfect for rabbit, and squirrel sized game, and can be set without a setting tool by most people. When setting these traps, it is a good idea to use a Safety Grip Tool, for your safety. These traps work by snapping shut with enough force to kill the animal with a blow to the neck, and they have enough power to break your hand if the trap is accidentally tripped while setting it.

Fishing Gear

One of the easiest and often most productive places to forage for food are in lakes and streams. While everyone knows about fishing with a pole, line, and hook, most people never consider methods such as trapping, spearing, gigging, or shooting fish (check your state's game and fish laws yadda, yadda, yadda) despite the fact that these methods are often far more effective.

First, let us talk about "fishing" after all this is the first thing that most people think of when "catching fish" is mentioned. It is easy to tie a line with hook and bait to a pole and toss the line into the water and wait for something to bite. Alternatively, to make a "hobo fishing reel" which is really just a soda, soup can or stick with fishing line wrapped around it. While this simple setup will not win any contests for "showiness", it can be put together in a couple of minutes and is effective enough to put food on the table if the fish are biting.

When riding an ATV or backpacking into the backcountry, I like to fish the abandoned farm ponds, and remote streams, that can be found in my area. I like to take a collapsible fishing rod or the voyager spinning travel kit with me, both work very well and don't get in the way when riding or hiking in wooded areas like a traditional fixed fishing rod would.

These types of rods will work great in a bug out kit and for foraging the waters away from your home or retreat after a disaster or TEOTWAWKI. Just be careful not to get so preoccupied with fishing that you become oblivious to your surroundings, and are taken by surprise by someone who may have bad intentions.

In this type of situation, after the stuff has hit the fan it is best not to go out alone if possible. When you're alone it's nearly impossible to do a task, such as fishing and stay 100% aware of your surroundings 100% of the time. Having an armed lookout, placed in a concealed location to watch your six is a good idea.

Ditto for other post-disaster, chores as well stay alert and if possible, post a lookout to watch your back...

For mobile fishing tackle, I keep it simple, a few assorted hooks, some split-shot sinkers, a few small artificial lures, and a couple small bobbers. This simple yet basic fishing gear is small and lightweight while still being effective for freshwater fish like bluegill and sunfish.

Another type of "fishing reel" that I have grown fond of using is the Yo Yo Fishing Reels. Several of these can be set and left alone while you go take care of other chores, like setting up camp or building a fire, and let's face it having several lines in the water at once can only increase your chances of catching something.

Edible Plants

Every prepper should be able to identify, harvest, and use the edible and medical plants that grow wild in their area. Luckily, there are a number of great books with color photos and detailed information on this subject, but like with most things you'll still need to go out and actually find, harvest and use these plants because nothing beats getting out in the field and doing it to gain lasting knowledge...

Two books that I recommend plus a video and deck of cards:

- The Forager's Harvest: A Guide to Identifying, Harvesting, and Preparing Edible Wild Plants by Samuel Thayer
- Backyard Foraging: 65 Familiar Plants You Didn't Know You Could Eat by Ellen Zachos
- Wild Cards: Edible Wild Foods available at Amazon.com

- The Forager's Harvest - Edible Wild Plants 2 DVD Set by Samuel Thayer

The following information on wild foods is contributed by Christine W and was first published at TheSurvivalistBlog.net.

I once read a very interesting article from a survivor of the Bosnian Collapse in the late 90's. This was a true end of the world as they knew it type of event, and it was fascinating and eye-opening to read. One of the things the man talked about in his extensive article was the most useful skills to possess. Medical knowledge was the highest on his list. Lacking real world medical training, people with the knowledge of the uses of herbs and plants were able to trade and use that knowledge to survive.

Most people in America cannot identify even 1% of the plants that surround them. They do not know useful from poisonous or nutritious from useless plants. Yet there are dozens of plants that grow even in urban settings that are not only edible but also downright lifesaving if you only can identify them. For 15 years, I have been a gardener and outdoorswoman. Much of my knowledge has come from being a curious person interested in the world around me, and from searching for natural ways to heal common ailments for my children and myself.

I have been amazed at the amount of plants growing near me that can be used for healing and have compiled a small list of what I consider the important common plants that grow in the USA, things you can find right out your back door. I am sure there are thousands more! Knowledge is power, so I recommend that you should start now when it comes to identifying wild and not so wild food and medicinal sources. Once you can recognize a plant start noting where you see them, what time of year they flower in your area, and when they bear fruit. I go out for drives along country roads and memorize where plants, bushes, berries, and helpful trees are growing.

You can also look around your neighborhood. Rose Bushes will provide you with rose hips that are high in vitamin C and can save you from scurvy in the winter. Echinacea also known as Purple Coneflowers are popular in gardens can boost the immune system and have a host of other uses. Look up color photos of plants on the internet to help you identify them, or join a wildcrafting group if one is available. Having a print out of each plant with multiple pictures and uses of them, along with how to use them and dosages, is very important in an SHTF event. There are many books specifying every area of America for finding wild foods and they often have excellent color pictures and identification keys. I keep a few of them in my purse when I go up to the wild and try to identify as many helpful plants as possible. Often these books are inexpensive so picking them up is a good idea.

As a note, I say where you can find the below plants. We live in the dry west so most plants only grow near water sources. However, I know that in other areas of the country rain is more plentiful so the growing habitat is much different. If you are gathering, post or during SHTF remember your personal safety and weigh the possible benefits vs. danger of running into other hungry people. Never go alone even now, as accidents happen and wild animals many times enjoy wild foods as much as people do. Meeting a hungry bear while picking berries is a highly unpleasant event! When you head to any wilderness, take precautions and let people know where you are going and when you are coming back. Always take a first aid kit, water, a good map, and some food with you.

Caution! As with any wild foraging check and double check your identification before eating anything, do not take another person's word on the safety of a plant. Some wild foods are debated on their safety, as some people will have a reaction where others do not. In addition, if you have food allergies be wary and careful when trying new things. Remember that when harvesting wild foods make sure they are not sprayed with poisons or chemicals. I am not a doctor and am not giving medical advice. If you want to try natural remedies, do your research and talk to your doctor. Even though these plants are natural, they can still be very strong medicines and even interact with other medication you are taking!

Alfalfa – Amazingly enough, this plant, a common feed for animals, is one of the most useful in a TEOTWAWKI collapse, or even just in a financial collapse where you suddenly become dirt poor. Alfalfa is highly nutritious and can be used to treat several conditions. The most important in my mind being bleeding, hemorrhaging, hemorrhaging after birth, and heavy menstrual bleeding. Blood loss is a common problem where medical care is limited and people are exposed to hard physical work or dangerous situations.

Childbirth for women is a often a fatal event in 3rd world countries, many of the deaths coming from hemorrhaging after birth. Drinking a tea made from alfalfa, or eating alfalfa in the last few weeks of pregnancy can help prevent hemorrhage or excessive bleeding due to several compounds it contains, this includes vitamin K, which is essential to blood clotting. I used this supplement under my midwife's supervision during my last two pregnancies.

My first two births went off well except that I hemorrhaged after birth. After my second birth, I hemorrhaged so severely that I was only saved by my midwife administering emergency shots of anti-hemorrhaging drugs (which will not be available to most women during and after a SHTF event). For two months after I was weaker than normal and under strict instructions to take it easy. My next two births went well and I barely bled at all, even compared to normal bleeding. Both times, I was taking alfalfa at the end of my pregnancy. Pregnant women should not take it until the last three weeks of pregnancy due to the fact that as it has hormone properties that could cause labor and miscarriage.

Once a woman is considered full term at 37 weeks that is not such an issue. Taking too much alfalfa for longer than a month can have the opposite effect and cause bleeding to be worse! Newborns need Vitamin K for proper development and usually receive an injection soon after birth, but during or after a SHTF event those shots may not be available and doctors recommend mothers consume foods with high vitamin K so that it will be passed to the nursing child. Dried or fresh alfalfa can be used in the human diet and as a compress on wounds to help them stop bleeding. In application to a wound, it is essential to boil the water for 10 minutes to kill bacteria and then boil the alfalfa added for a few minutes thus killing any bacteria on the plant leaves. Alfalfa helps people who are nutritionally deficient.

It helps a great deal with vitamin C deficiency when used fresh, for it contains more vitamin C than some citrus fruits. Scurvy is caused by a vitamin C deficiency and is a common problem for people during famines, or when there is a lack of fresh fruits and vegetables. It also has very high B vitamin levels and Vitamin D levels, which help with problems such as rickets, a common disease especially affecting children who have poor diets or are not exposed to enough sunlight. This is a common problem when living in a war zone or an area where people must stay inside much of the time due to violence as Vitamin D cannot be manufactured by the body and is mainly created by the skins exposure to the sun.

Alfalfa is also easy to store when dried and is very cheap. It is a good item to keep on hand. Alfalfa is grown everywhere in the USA and can be found along ditch banks and country roads growing wild, in fields, as well as in farmyards. It does not need to be reseeded every year so a field that had it last year will have it this year as well.

Raspberry Leaf – Raspberries (also known as redcaps, brambleberries, dewberry, and thimbleberry) grow wild in the USA and are even considered an invasive species. They come in red, black, purple, and golden fruit all of which is essentially the same plant, but these other fruit colors do not generally grow in the wild as the common red does. Obviously, the fruit is edible but the leaves and even roots can be used for highly effective remedies.

The most well-known is for aid to painful menstruation, to regulate and normalize a woman's cycle, and also to help shorten and lessen the pain of childbirth. I am all for shortening the length of childbirth; having had four children naturally! Caution must be used however as a raspberry leaf can cause uterine contractions, so it should only be used once labor has begun or a week before birth is expected.

It can be used by non-pregnant women during and right before menstruation. Another equally important use of raspberry leaf is its use as a cure for diarrhea. More on that in the Blackberry Section. These plants are found near water, in boggy areas, besides stream banks, in gullies, on ditch banks, or growing anywhere that gets plentiful rainfall.

Blackberry Fruits, Leaves, and Roots – Diarrhea is one of the most common killers in third world countries due to contaminated water supplies and poor water treatment facilities. As a country collapses the infrastructure of water treatment always breaks down, and waterborne illness explodes. Preparation for such disease is essential when we plan for a SHTF event.

Diarrhea is especially fatal to children and the elderly and is frightening at how fast it kills. Soldiers in battle frequently suffer from dysentery due to bad water as well. For century's blackberries (and to a lesser extent any of the bramble berry varieties such a red caps, black caps, Marion berries, dewberries, and raspberries) have been used for treating diarrhea, dysentery, foodborne illness, and even the more deadly waterborne illnesses. This must be remembered to be a treatment, not a cure as diarrhea is a symptom of an infection in the body, which must be treated as well.

Blackberry Root Bark is the most effective remedy for diarrhea, but if you cannot get to the roots the leaves are highly effective as well, even dried ones. Last is the fruit, which can be eaten, or a syrup or juice made from the fruit. A syrup or juice is especially useful when treating small children. One teaspoon of root or leaves per boiling cup of water, steeped for 20 minutes, then sweetened with honey, if possible, due to its healing and soothing properties is a good dosage. The tannins in the blackberry plant help with diarrhea. Blackberries are even more invasive than red raspberries and grow profusely throughout the USA. If in a dry region, look for them along streams or down in gullies and canyons. The leaves and root bark are easy to dry, and the leaves can be eaten and are high in nutrition.

Elderberries – I grew up eating wild elderberries; these are round purple-ish blue fruit that grows in clusters on a bushy tree. The bushes flower in late spring depending on your area and the fruits are ripe in early fall. They are very common growing wild and like water so they grow either near water sources or in areas that get plenty of rain. I often see them growing in old farmyards or homesteads because the pioneers and old farmers used them not only for health but also as a much-needed fruit. They also can be found in gullies and draws. The fruit has a dusty powder on it, but care should be taken as the red elderberry, the stems of all elderberries that connect to the fruit, and also the unripe fruit, are poisonous.

The fruit and flowers have been proven in clinical trials to help with many ailments, but especially in respiratory infections such as bronchitis and to help thin mucus. The fruit is very high in vitamin C and is used to treat the flu and to boost the immune system. Elderberries would be good for an insurance against scurvy.

161

Harvesting is easy and making juice, syrups, or tinctures from them is the best way to use them for healing.

The flowers are used to make a tea or tincture for respiratory ailments and compresses for wounds. They also are good in pies, jams, jellies, and to make wine, and liquors. There is some evidence that they should be cooked before consuming as uncooked raw fruit can cause stomach upset. Elderberry syrup is safe for children.

Other Berries – Obviously, there are many berries growing throughout the United States, many of them not only edible but beneficial as well. Getting a good book on berry identification for your area is an excellent idea.

Rosehips – Wild roses grow all over the USA along roads, up in the mountains, and in forests. They are usually found as just a single flower, meaning they are a single layer of petals in a ring around the central part of the flower, maybe five petals in a ring. Roses are also grown in many yards and gardens, and there are even rose varieties grown specifically for large rosehips. Rosehips are the main and most helpful part of the plant for use. Wild roses have small hips compared to their cultivated cousins, but size does not matter when it comes to food and medicinal value.

They can be eaten raw in a pinch, but the most common way is to chop the hips roughly and pour 1 cup boiling water over two teaspoons of the chopped hips. Allow them to steep for 20 minutes and sweeten with honey or, if for a child less than two years of age, sugar, or syrup. Rose hips are higher in vitamin C than citrus fruit and not only prevent, but treat scurvy.

They are easy to identify and easy to harvest. Rose hips make a tea that is tart and pleasant to drink. They can help treat urinary tract infections and the flu, and rose hips boost the immune system. When fresh veggies and fruit are unavailable, rosehips can be found even in winter and still eaten as they do not rot easily, and cling to the rosebush. Rosehips are generally a reddish color, and it is wise to look for ones that are still firm, not black or with mold or rot on them. They can be used to make syrup, jelly, jam, wine, and juice. The flowers of roses are also edible but make sure you do not eat them if they are been sprayed with pesticide.

<u>Bachelor Buttons</u> – Bachelor Buttons, also known as cornflowers, are a flower that grows wild and cultivated across the USA. They are popular in wildflower or cottage gardens, are also drought tolerant, and reseed prolifically in the wild. The common color is a cobalt blue, but especially in gardens, they come in white, light pink, and purple. The flower is the part used and is most commonly utilized as an eyewash for injured or infected eyes. This is usually done by steeping the flowers in freshly boiled water, cooled, and then applied over the eyes on a moistened rag.

A similar wash for cuts and sores in the mouth aids healing. In this instance, it is best to spit out after swishing around the mouth. Furthermore, they can also be used in the same form to wash cuts, scrapes, and bruises. Combine one teaspoon of dried cornflower petals, or five fresh blossoms with one cup of boiling water. Cover and steep for 15-20 minutes; after this, you may strain and consume. If taking internally, it is best for no longer than two weeks. Cornflower tea has been used to calm diarrhea, treat urinary tract infections, and for anxiety or nervousness. This flower is usually found along roadsides, in fields, and in clearings. They love full sun and they are very easy to grow. Women who are pregnant or breastfeeding should not use this internally. If you have allergies to daisies or ragweed, you should not use this at all.

<u>Lambs Quarters/Wild Spinach</u> – Lambs Quarters, also known as wild spinach, goosefoot, pigweed, good king henry, and fat hen, is considered by most gardeners as a weed, but is, in fact, is a highly nutritious and delicious plant that grows everywhere and is easy to identify. It is nicer than common spinach because it is slow to bolt

in the heat of summer, and because while tasting like spinach, it is, even more, nutritious. It can be cooked or eaten raw and the stems leaves and seeds are all edible. It can also be frozen, canned, or dried for later eating. Lamb's Quarters is a good survival food and can be found in yards, abandoned lots, fields, gardens, and along roads. You can cut it off almost to the root, yet it comes up and starts leafing out again.

Dandelion – Dandelion is another common yard weed that grows almost everywhere, including in the mountains. I never dig up the dandelions in my yard but use them and also feed them to our rabbits. We do not treat our yard with chemicals. It is highly nutritious, and all parts are edible- including the roots, which can be dried and used as a coffee substitute. It has been used as a diuretic and to cleanse the blood of toxins. The milk that comes when you cut the plant can be used on wounds and is highly effective to use on warts. I have used the milk on three of my children's warts and all three times, it made them disappear naturally without pain or scarring. It must be applied every day until healed. A tea made from all parts of the dandelion is absurdly rich in nutrients and would be well utilized by those suffering from malnutrition.

Wild Onions – Wild onions are easy to identify because they smell like onions! They are considered a weed in many parts of the country, and they can be eaten like regular onions while being a healthy addition to the diet and are easy to dry for future use. They can be in yards or near places that have a constant water supply or a good rain.

Pine Trees/Spruce Trees – Pine trees are common all across the USA and several parts of the tree can be used both medicinally and nutritionally. The needles themselves are rich in vitamin C and can be steeped in boiling water to create a tea to fight scurvy (vitamin C deficiency), and they are also high in vitamin A and beta-carotene.

Spruce tip tea or pine needle tea is useful to treat a sore throat, cough, colds, and chest congestion. This is a very important survival food as it is so readily available and easy to find. The best tasting needles are young tender ones, but older needles work just the same nutritionally. Pine nuts that are found in pinecones are rich in calories, healthy fats, vitamins, and minerals and are high in vitamin K which helps stop bleeding. The inner bark of pine trees is even edible but should only be used in an emergency because to get at it, you will kill the tree.

Pine Sap has many uses and is highly effective for use on wounds when mixed as a salve to prevent and treat infection. It is also used as a flu and cold treatment when mixed with honey, or made into a tincture. It not only fights the infection inside but also soothes sore throats.

Chopped pine needles added to a hot bath can help with skin problems since they contain natural sulfur, they also soothe sore muscles and joints. Pine oil can be used by adding a few drops to boiling water and then breathing in the steam; there is evidence that it helps cure sinus infections, bronchitis, and breaks up mucus. Pine oil kills germs and can be used to clean surfaces during illnesses, although, it must always be diluted and never applied straight to skin.

However, pine oil is a distilled product and must go through special processing and may not be easy to replicate after SHTF (although what a skill to have!) Use roughly chopped pine needles, with boiling water poured over, then cover your head with a towel over the bowl and breathe deeply. Pine needles are also a natural flea and bug repellent and can be used to stuff beds and cushions to deter them. The scent of pine is generally very calming. Caution – Pregnant women should not use pine needle tea, as there is fear it could cause miscarriage. There are three varieties of toxic pine, and it is highly recommended to learn how to identify and avoid them. They are Norfolk Island pine, Yew, and Ponderosa Pine.

Crabapples – These are a variety of apple that is often overlooked as an edible fruit because they are unpleasant for fresh eating. They are very good for cooking and if sweetened can be made into pies, jams, jellies, syrup, wine, pickled, and when mixed with other fruits dried in fruit leather. They were mainly used by our ancestors as an addition to cider making as they added depth of flavor and a bit of tartness to the finished product. There are many varieties of crabapple tree and the fruit can be quite large as they are grown for their pretty look.

They are grown in many yards and businesses as a decorative tree and the fruit is most often left to rot. Most people I have asked are eager to let me pick off their trees since otherwise they eventually fall and have to be raked up. They also can be found growing wild and in old orchards or farms. Crabapples are high in vitamin C and make a pleasant tea when sweetened. They have been used to treat urinary infections and can be juiced to make cider vinegar, which is one of the healthiest things you can make. For the best flavor harvest after they have been frosted on.

Wild Plums – These are native to the USA and grow in all parts. They are small and are usually a yellowish red color. Wild Plums are a tasty fruit for fresh eating and are useful in making jam, jelly, syrup, pies, and pickles. They are very high in vitamin C and Iron. Dried or fresh they are a good laxative and treat anemia.

Cattails – A well-known wild food that grows in marshy or wet areas these are easy to identify. All parts of the plant are edible in different seasons and have good food value. The root can be pounded and applied to cuts and scrapes as a poultice. As these always grown near or in water, be careful of pollution.

166

Rhubarb – This is not necessarily a wild food but it is so common that noting where it grows is a good idea. This plant comes back year after year for practically ever and you see it often in abandoned lots, old farmsteads, abandoned homes, or in people's gardens. Most people never use it and are happy to give away to those who will. Harvesting in the spring is best when it is tender. Rhubarb can be made into jam, sauce, syrup, put into pies, cakes, and bread, and canned. Rhubarb is rich in B- complex vitamins such as folates, riboflavin, niacin, vitamin B-6, thiamin, and pantothenic acid and good levels of vitamin K. It has been used to treat stomach problems. The leaves are poisonous, only the stalks should be eaten.

Daylilies – These grow all over the US and in many places, they grow wild or have taken over lots of land and gardens, as they are hardy and invasive. They are edible. The shoots when young in spring can be cooked like asparagus or eaten raw, the flowers should be harvested in summer and can be fried as if squash flowers, chopped and added to salads, and immature buds cooked like green beans. The tubers can be gathered year round and cooked like corn. They have been used to treat arsenic poisoning.

Nuts – So many trees produce edible nuts that all I can recommend is that you get a good identification book and start looking around you. Nuts are high in nutrition, healthy fats, and calories so they make an excellent survival food. A couple of varieties that are overlooked by people are acorns and pine nuts found in pinecones. Acorns have good food value but are bitter so most people avoid them, meaning that you will have more opportunity to gather them. Learn how to process them to get out the bitterness.

Wild Strawberries – Also known as Alpine strawberry, Common Strawberry, Mountain Strawberry, Pineapple Strawberry, Wild Strawberries, Wood Strawberry, Woodland strawberry. These grow prolifically all over the USA and although the fruit is very nice to eat (but tiny), the leaves have great food value and have been used to treat diarrhea when made into a tea. The leaves contain beneficial minerals and vitamins. The root is also used to treat diarrhea. These like shady places but also can grow in sunny clearings and fields.

Wild Violets – The leaves and the flowers are edible and can be found growing in many yards and gardens where they are considered a weed. They are purple-ish blue or white and can be found in the shade of forests or moist clearings. They can be added to salads or cooked. The medicinal uses are many and they make a lovely salve for irritated skin and rashes and a tea can be made from the leaves and flowers to ease the pain of headaches and arthritis as well as to treat diarrhea. They appear early in spring and grow all summer long in the shade. They are loaded with vitamin A and C, which makes them a good remedy for colds and flu. The flowers can be added to jellies during the cooking stage and turn the liquid a lovely violet color.

Ferns – Several fern varieties are edible and are often called fiddleheads; however, care must be taken, as there are also several non-edible varieties that can cause mild to severe illness. Invest in a good identification book or print many pictures out of edible varieties off the internet for better identification. These must be harvested in early to late spring. They are fried, steamed sautéed, boiled, and pickled and are rich in vitamin A and C.

Wild Greens – There are so many kinds that it would take a good-sized book to describe them all and I highly recommend buying a field guide and searching them out. Some that are common and worth investigating are mustard, watercress, stinging nettle, miners lettuce, sorrel, red clover, and sweet coltsfoot. Most greens are best harvested in the spring and early summer when they are tender and young.

Willow Tree – The willow tree has been used for thousands of years to treat pain. It grows in yards and woods across the United States. The bark of the tree, especially that of the White Willow tree is what as used and has the same actions of aspirin for treating pain and fever Use 1 to 2 teaspoons of willow bark to 8 oz of boiling water and boil for 5 to 10 minutes. Then turn off heat and allow steeping for 20 to 30 minutes more. Drinking 3 to 4 cups throughout the day is recommended to be effective. Gathering and drying the bark in spring summer and fall would be a good idea to have a store through winter. This is a real medication similar in its side effects to aspirin; it interacts with several drugs and can cause the same stomach problems as aspirin so research it well before use. Pregnant and nursing women and children under two should never use willow bark.

Mints – Mints are not a wild species but are so highly invasive once planted in a garden that they quickly spread and can take over vast tracts of land. There are many varieties and just as many uses both as a food as well as medicinally. Mints are high in vitamin A and spearmint, in particular, is high in minerals. It is often used internally to treat stomach upset, headaches, body aches, reduce fever, for sore throats and cough, anti-flatulence, and diarrhea. Externally mint is an excellent insect repellent and can be used to treat lice, muscle aches, and soothe insect bites, hair care, and vaginitis. A simple tea is used internally and is quite pleasant; externally a similar tea can be made and cooled before application.

Mushrooms – Wild mushrooms can be very helpful both medicinally and nutritionally but great care must be taken, as so many varieties are deadly. I will not go into them here but invest in a good full-color photographic field guide, and even then be careful! The only mushroom I feel very safe harvesting is morels because they are so distinctive and only have one similar species to contend with. As my father said, they look like a brain!

<u>Tree Saps</u> – Several trees produce edible saps that can be boiled down into sweet syrups. Most commonly, we think of the maple tree, and all maples produce sap although the sugar maple is the most well-known and produces the highest volume per tree.

There are however several other trees that produce good sap for human use. Pine trees are one but the sap is more for medicinal use than for pleasurable eating. Birch, Walnut, and Sycamore all produce an edible sap for syrup making. Obviously, these are high in sugar content, which equals calories. As a caution only, stick to the above or other documented non-poisonous trees for sap. Tree sap syrup has many vitamins and minerals making them a good survival food.

<u>Wild Leeks Or Ramps</u> – These are a leek or onion-like bulb that are common throughout the United States in forested areas and grow often near streams or on hills. The leaves when torn or bruised smell of onion or garlic so they are easy to identify. The plant resembles lily of the valley. These are found and harvested in the spring. When harvesting only take half of what you find so they can continue to propagate.

<u>Supplies For Harvesting</u> – A good pair of boots and weather specific clothing, good identification books or literature, a small hand shovel, a good sturdy bucket/basket with a handle/or canvas bags, a knife for cutting, gardening gloves, a sidearm for meetings with predators of the four-legged to two-legged kind.

Chapter 13

BARTER ITEMS

I added this chapter last because stock-piling barter items should be last on your list of priorities, not because it's "unimportant" but because you should get the rest of the items and skills that are detailed above first, and only then should you start investing in barter items and items to retain wealth like gold and silver.

In a post collapse world the only economy maybe a barter economy, with currency having little or no value if this is the case then look for the value of certain things like sewing needles, animal traps, ammo, and matches, for example, could increase dramatically.

Put back what you will need for your own survival first, then and only after ensuring that you have enough survival supplies such as food, water, water filters, first-aid, fuel, weapons, and ammunition etc., to meet your own needs should you worry about stocking up on trade items.

Skills

Develop your survival skills and knowledge. Your skills and knowledge may be your biggest asset when it comes to trade during an economic collapse or societal breakdown. Medical skills are the first to come to mind. Doctors, EMT'S, nurses, and other medically trained individuals will be in high demand. Other related skills include dentists, herbalists, and veterinarians.

The ability to build shelters, garden, set up and run a distillery, hunting, and trapping, collecting and purifying water, gun repair, reloading, blacksmith, butcher, baker, and candlestick maker. Any skill filling a need for a number of people would be an asset and a valuable trade commodity.

Having useful skills maybe the best barter item, you could ever have, and it is a renewable resource!

Gold And Silver

There are a lot of financial advisers and survival authors that suggest putting back gold and silver to use as barter items after an economic collapse, and I agree, just do not go overboard here. It is important to get your other lifesaving preps in order first, before worrying about investing in gold, or silver.

Get out of debt. The first thing that you want to get paid off is you property and home. Having five to ten acres of paid-off property, where you can raise a garden, chickens, rabbits, goats and bees is the most important survival prep that you can make.

Gold and silver are a good hedge against the property tax because gold and silver hold their value fairly well, it would be an easy matter to sell enough of either to pay the property tax or even pay it directly to the county with the metals in some cases.

CBMint and JM Bullion have huge inventories and with competitive prices and fast shipping...

Ammunition

Some think ammunition would be a great barter item after the crash. If you can keep from being shot with your own wares then robbed, then ammunition would be a great trade item. The thing is people are selfish and could decide it would be more productive for them just to shoot you and take what you have.

Robbery and murder are commonplace during normal times; one can only imagine how bad it would become in the days after a major social breakdown. If you decide to put away ammunition for barter purposes, my advice is to put back .22 Rimfire rounds and trade only with people you know and trust.

Hand Tools

Hand tools such as saws, hammers, drills, knives, ax heads and handles, shovels, garden hoes and other tools will be in great demand after a collapse, the problem becomes the financing. Tools cost money; even the cheaper quality items will set you back a hefty amount if you try laying back a significant quality. Pawn shops are a good place to look for deals on hand tools.

Whiskey and Cigarettes

Whiskey and Cigarettes would become very valuable items if the normal supply were suddenly stopped. You would have little trouble trading these items for just about anything needed. Just do not get arrested by the BATF, do not think for a moment that the government will go away just because of an economic or another long-term disaster, no way. The powers that set on the throne will only strengthen its grip on the population, becoming more suppressive to stay in control.

Animal Traps

Putting back extra animal traps like live traps, and snares for barter is a good idea, however do not go overboard with this, because most people will not know how to use them correctly and if they do then they will probably be competing with you for available food resources by setting up and trapping animals in your area.

I hope that you have enjoyed this book and found it useful but most of all I hope that you will put the information that I have given you to good use...

Remember:

A prudent person foresees danger and takes precautions. The simpleton goes blindly on and suffers the consequences. Proverbs 22:3

ABOUT THE AUTHOR

M.D. Creekmore is a full-time survival author and emergency preparedness consultant and is the owner and editor at TheSurvivalistBlog.net. He is also the author of three other books including - 31 Days to Survival, Dirt Cheap Survival Retreat, and The Prepared Prepper's Cookbook.

Over the years, he has studied all facets of survivalism and has learned what works and, more importantly, what does not. His books are based on first-hand real-world experience.

Qualifications Include

- Being a certified gunsmith
- Certified in CPR / First Aid / AED
- Completed FEMA courses Leadership & Influence, Effective Communications, and Are You Ready? An In-Depth Guide to Citizen Preparedness
- Tennessee handgun training completed
- KY hunter education completed
- Over 25 years hunting, trapping, outdoor, and shooting experience
- A dedicated student of military history and small unit tactics
- A dedicated student of collapsed civilizations
- He is a second-degree black belt in Shotokan Karate
- He has been homeless and lived in a tent for several months (Personal SHTF event and a learning experience)
- He lived completely off the power grid for over three years in a travel trailer
- He is a jack-of-all-trades handyman
- Over 20 years prepping experience

- He currently, own and operate a 5 1/2 acre homestead in TN
- He has been interviewed and consulted as a content expert for American Survival Guide Magazine
- He has written articles for Survivalist Magazine.
- He been mentioned in and online at Mother Earth News and Backwoods Home magazines
- He has also been referenced in hundreds of online blogs, forums, and websites and in several books by other authors

If you have comments or questions, the author can be contacted via his website at www.thesurvivalistblog.net

Made in the USA
Las Vegas, NV
03 October 2024

96127927R00098